Love Marriage and the Art of Raising Children

How to Find Love and Make It Last
Book II

Includes The 101 Question Compatibility Test

Virginia C. Gleser

Copyright 2018
Published by Harmony Publishing, A Division of Sky Sail Productions
512 14th Street
Modesto, Ca. 95354
Join me: Virginia Gleser (author) on Facebook

First printing of *Love, Marriage and the Art of Raising Children*, Buenos Aires, Argentina. 2005
Second revised edition, *How to Find Love and Make It Last, A Practical Guide to Relationships, Includes the 101 Question Compatibility Test.* Book 1, United States, 2016.
Love, Marriage and the Art of Raising Children, How to Find Love and Make It Last, Book II United States, 2018

All rights reserved. No portion of this book may be reproduced by any means whatsoever, without written permission from the publisher, except for brief quotations in reviews.

Love, Marriage and the Art of Raising Children, How to Find Love and Make It Last, Book II
Virginia C. Gleser
ISBN# 978-0-964-7247-5-4

The typeface used for the text of this book is Cambria

What People are saying about *How To Find Love and Make It Last, A Practical Guide to Relationships.*

A Must Read for everyone who wants a Lasting Loving Relationship. I recommend this book to everyone who wants to improve their current relationship and those looking for a lasting one. The book is well crafted with great information interwoven with the author's personal journey. This is a good reference for young adults looking to find their life partner. The self-improvement chapters to aid in changing bad habits and actions are ones I will refer to often. The 101 questions are very good and the "answers" give insight to the process. This would be a good book for a high school or college health or relationship class. (Phil Rink, author of **Jimi & Isaac Books for kids**)

Where was this book 40-some years ago when my husband and I were dating? The 101 Question Compatibility Test alone is worth the price of the book. The questions sparked some good conversations even now after decades of marriage. Virginia Gleser offers insights and anecdotes from her own relationship, and the advice she gives is wise and realistic. She has excellent tips for better communication, whether you're talking about values, money, religion, in-laws, - or anything that can turn into a tense moment or a fight. The book is a must read for anyone thinking about marriage, or for that matter, anyone looking for a better marriage. (Janelle Diller – author, *The Pack n Go Girls Adventure Series, Never Enough Flamingos, Never Enough Sisters, Never Enough Lilacs Trilogy*)

I loved your book very much especially Changes, Karma, Surrender, Forgiveness, Positive Thinking. I've been learning about life, thinking that no one else would understand what I was going through which is all of the above. And now I know just about everyone will go through it one day and it's a part of life and growing up!
-Jennifer Caswell

I am a teacher and want to use some of your book in my class like "Making Changes," but I also realized the book was even more beneficial to me. -Valerie Stewart

I want to give your book to all of my family and friends. The Tool Box for communication is excellent and I keep it by my bed. -Terry McGuffin

To Robert: Living our dreams and sharing your adventuresome spirit in our ever-evolving marriage has filled me with happiness. I have a never-ending appreciation for your commitment to continually go through the difficult changes that have made you into the wonderful partner that you are. I wake up every morning looking forward to your hugs and sweet words of love.

Table of Contents

Love, Marriage and the Art of Raising Children, Sequel to: How To Make Love Last

Introduction 1

Part 1. Marriage 14
Your Wedding Day 14
The Art of Marriage 15
A Supportive Family and Community 16
The Honeymoon 17
The Art of Making Love 18
The "One" 21
After the Honeymoon 23
Are You a Good Partner? 25
Our Commitment is Tested 27
Tools for Creating the Love You Want 29
The Subconscious 33
Ten Steps to Illuminate the 40
Subconscious 40
Communication 43
An Updated Robert's Rules of Order 44
Tools for Your Communication Toolbox 45
Karma and Personal Responsibility 61
Feedback 63
Uh, Oh, Negative Habits 66
Forgive and Let Go 69
Catch Me Exercise 74
Perspective Counts 75
Careers and Finances: Is Your Work Fulfilling? 77
Cooperative Finances 80
 The Power Struggle 90
Drawing the Line 93
You Did What? You had an Affair? 97
Breaking Up is Hard to Do 101

Joint Custody and a Single-Parent Home 103
Keeping the Romance Hot 105

Part 2. The Art of Raising Children 108
Mahatma Gandhi, a "Householder Yogi" 112
The Birthing -- Welcome to the Planet 114
The Newborn 118
Infants 126
Weaning Your Baby 128
The Challenging Twos 129
Potty-Training 133
Babysitting 134
Discipline 136
Screen Time 142
Learning Disabilities 145
The Preschool Years 147
The Elementary School Years 151
Middle School 158
A Family Meeting 161
The Teenage Years 163
The Rite of Passage 173
The Roaring Twenties 174
A Return to the Big World 177
The Empty Nest 180

Part 3: Taking the Test 182
The 101 Question Compatibility Test 183
How did The Test Go for You? 191

Acknowledgments 192
Appendix A:
Reading References by Subject 194
Bibliography 200
Endnotes 204
More Books By Virginia Gleser 214

Love, Marriage and the Art of Raising Children, Sequel to: How to Find Love and Make It Last

Introduction

When my teenage children were attending high school and beginning to date, I stayed up late writing this guide to help them travel the labyrinth of love with their eyes wide open. I hoped that understanding the difficult lessons my husband, Robert and I had learned during our then thirty years of marriage (now 47), and the subsequent changes we had gone through, could help them make intelligent choices when they were looking for partners. I wanted to shine a light on how to build a vibrant, ever-evolving union. It soon became obvious that I was writing for everyone, not just my kids, and especially for those of you who have been through tough times in previous relationships and are still looking for that special someone. I wanted to write the book I wish I had read when I was beginning to explore the erotic and mysterious world of dating, and later on when I was married and having children. I read my trusted Dr. Spock, but wanted more.

It wasn't until our children had flown the nest, and Robert and I were spending the summer of 2005 in Buenos Aires, Argentina that I finally had time to publish *Love, Marriage, and the Art of Raising Children*. Small print shops abound in this vibrant city, and we found a competent printer with a Heidelberg press and a layout team to make my book a reality. With a favorable exchange rate, it fit in our budget to make a short run of 250 copies. Of course, this was right before Amazon and others made self-publishing affordable.

Our kids (believe it or not) found my manuscript useful when they were searching for their life partners. They were also kind enough to circulate it among their friends and I began to receive positive feedback. It felt great when a high school teacher actually used my book in her life skills class, and sent me precious letters from her students about how much it had meant to them. She wrote that she actually needed it as much as her students.

The enthusiastic response inspired me to release an updated and renamed edition, *How to Find Love and Make It Last, A Practical Guide to Relationships, Includes: The 101 Question Compatibility Test, Book 1* and *Love, Marriage and the Art of Raising Children, How to Find Love and Make It Last, Book II.* I have divided the manuscript into two books since it addresses different stages of life. Book 1 covers such topics as Finding "The One," Tools for Communication, Dating, Safety First, Loving Yourself, and How to Change Your Contrary Habits in order to transform yourself into a wonderful partner. The 101 Question Compatibility Test is followed by 101 Answers that explore each issue in more depth. Book II includes chapters on how to make marriage a sparkling life-long adventure and how raising children is an awesome and life affirming experience. A copy of the Compatibility Test is included in Book II, as well as a few relevant chapters from Book 1 like The Communication Toolbox, The Subconscious, and Forgive and Let Go that are valuable for every stage of life.

Love is an action word. I would like to take you on an exploratory journey into the intricacies of love: to the psychic frontier where you can find truth through communication, and where you can clean out old resentments, apologize for hurts, forgive past wrongs, dump mental garbage and unload childhood pain. With a clear and open heart, mind, and body, you'll be prepared for a relationship that can operate in prime running condition.

> **Love is an action word.**

Love, Marriage and the Art of Raising Children and How to Find Love and Make It Last, Book 1 and Book 2 are a Driver's Ed manual to help you negotiate the, often, elusive route to a successful relationship. Our culture has a love affair with cars and in California for instance, the general requirements for a driver's license are a written test and a vision check-up. Then you receive a permit, which qualifies you to take a training course before taking the final driving exam. It is easy to make a mistake during the road test, and many nervous drivers fail the exam at least once. When you do receive your license, you gain the privilege to join the large community out on the road.

When it comes to love, marriage, and parenting, unfortunately, there are no required classes, tests, practice hours, or reality checks that might help assure a successful relationship. It is not surprising that statistics give a married couple around a 60% chance of success.[1] It appears that there is a social crisis, and the children suffer along with their parents. Can we stem the flood?

These days, four out of ten marriages fail, which is, believe it or not, better than previous decades, when it was closer to 50%. Also, single parents work double time to keep it together in one out of every four households, and unwanted pregnancies are still too common.[2]

A bright light does shine. Despite these unfavorable odds, statistics have improved, and there continues to be beautifully raised children with co-parenting and blended families of all sorts. These are parents who realize that caring for a child is a marathon and not a sprint, a dedicated, life-long, ever evolving adventure.

Mental and emotional issues caused by family upheavals add undo stress to young peoples' lives. When problems are addressed and sorted out instead of left on the back burner to build up pressure, everyone can thrive.

With a commitment for self-improvement and personal responsibility, perhaps we can create a large societal paradigm shift. Equipped with relevant tools for communication, you can become aware of what it takes to have a successful relationship and avoid repeating those old destructive patterns. By delving into the ways a happy relationship works, - physically, emotionally, and spiritually, - as well as what it takes to have love stick around year after year, you can create a romance that is vibrant and full of joy.

When you find that deep, long-lasting connection, there's a special feeling that only happens around true love. You wake up in the morning to warm hugs and whispers of how much you love each other. An easygoing communication exists and you can talk about anything and everything, especially about problems that would ordinarily cause hassles. When you share cooking, gardening, dancing, laughter, travel and adventure or whatever it is that you love to do, you are surrounded by happiness and your horizons expand. Of course, lovemaking is a beautiful time to connect and reach an intimacy that is healing to body, mind and spirit. Your work is also inspiring and you bring home enthusiasm to share with your partner. Life is not stagnant or boring but continually evolving with exciting new discoveries and experiences, both inward and outward. The essence of your loving relationship is a deep respect for your partner, unobstructed communication, and a willingness to change. It feels like you've won the lottery; dreams become reality, magic happens, and love soars.

> **The essence of your relationship is a deep respect for your partner, unobstructed communication, and a willingness to change.**

Life can actually be like this, but rarely in the real world does an idyllic, contention-free relationship just happen. When trouble comes, often the old "fight or flight response" kicks in, and it might seem easier to run away, fight back, or give up. One or both of you may have reached the point where you have dug in your heels and refused to make a change. Having a peaceful discussion about your thoughts and feelings can be next to impossible when the air is full of tension, and neither of you seems to be listening. Sometimes, compromises are difficult to achieve, and both of you may feel stuck in a passionless void. To remain together "for the children," usually becomes an unhealthy choice if a foundation for a workable partnership has not been created. Inevitably frustration, anger, depression, and at the worst, domestic violence can deteriorate into a poisonous relationship. With today's statistics, marriage looms as a risky proposition. The divorce rate is proof that what we have done up until now could use some improvement. If our society is to survive with a balanced state of mind and a contented spirit, then we need to find a way to build and nurture successful relationships.

Unfortunately, the fallout of separation and divorce often lands unevenly on the woman's shoulders and, sadly, rains down on the children. Although women have made incredible advances in lifting the glass ceiling, there is still a 16% discrepancy in equal pay for equal work.[3] If there are children, the mother is often left with the responsibility of raising them, although joint custody arrangements are becoming the norm. Also, the security, trust, and comfort, found in a home where two people love and respect each other is gone.

     Currently, many young people are living together and shying away from the formal marriage agreement. Is the necessary commitment present if children enter the picture? The pressures of parenting can overwhelm a couple, from lack of sleep, to keeping up with the bills, and there's often little time or energy to spend quality time with your partner. It is at this point where the agreement, formally declared in front of your family and friends, can serve as a protective bubble around you, even while it is being tested. Count yourself lucky if you have a supportive family that can help with the inevitable stresses that surface in a new partnership. I wish I had been given some clues about what a marriage truly entails and what to expect. A few tools for how to communicate would have come in handy.

     Love, Marriage and the Art of Raising Children, How to Find Love and Make It Last, Book II is an in depth guide on how to create a romantic, and ever-evolving long-term relationship, while manifesting a sane, healthy, and happy environment in which to raise your children. Included is a set of tools to deal with the inevitable challenges that confront all of us. The *101 Question Compatibility Test* is also included, bringing up common situations that might arise as a relationship develops. With practical insights into what to expect, you are on your way to finding compromises when the inevitable disagreements pop up. You can refer to *The Answers* in Book 1 that delve further into the specifics, revealing what changes you can make to help maintain a long-term commitment. Lucky in Love happens when preparation meets opportunity.[4]

***

Everyone is brought up on fairy tales about the Handsome Young Prince and the Lovely Princess. The radiant couple, after many trials and tribulations, continues on to have a glorious wedding, accompanied by dazzling sunbeams and birds' sweet songs. The celebrated couple walks hand in hand into the sunset, and then what? Is it happily ever after, or does the sun go down and it gets dark, in a real and metaphorical sense? The seed of the union has been planted in the fertile earth. The sun then shines and the rain falls beckoning the plants to reach upwards. With love and nurturing, the marriage can become a connected, deeply rooted family. And then, inevitably, reality sets in, life has its ups and downs, and no one seems to be immune from the struggles. Does a new couple have any idea what to expect when it comes to keeping the spark of love alive?

> **Lucky in Love happens when preparation meets opportunity.**

Considering the high divorce rate, the answer seems to be a resounding No! It is painful for everyone to see marriages fall apart. Not only is there the sadness and anger that a couple feels from having attempted to create a successful relationship that didn't work out, but there are also the deep conflicting emotions of the children who have had their world turned upside-down. Researcher Nicholas Wolfinger found that the children of broken families are more likely to go through a divorce than people who were raised by intact families.[5] Unfortunately, their experiences have left them with distorted lessons about love, trust, respect, commitment, mutual sacrifice, and fidelity.

When the heart closes down, love stops, and hard work is required to rekindle the spark. When there is bickering and hassling (of which Robert and I, unfortunately, have had plenty of experience), the energy is sucked out of the room and love flies out the window. When you do the work to unblock old destructive patterns, it leads to true love, and an enduring marriage filled with passion, good times, and more than a few miracles. A functioning family is the inevitable product of a couple whose priorities are a commitment to love each other and keep the pathways to happiness free from obstructions.

Before the baby-boomer generation came of age, the number of divorces was extremely low, mainly because it was financially, culturally, socially, and religiously unacceptable.[6] These marriages were not necessarily happy unions.[7]

Wives sometimes stayed with their partners under terrible conditions of abuse, drunkenness, and infidelity. Later, when the liberation movement came along, women realized that they didn't have to live under tyranny at home or in the workplace. For the first time, many women were capable of earning enough at their jobs to survive adequately on their own.

Embracing their recent liberation and independence, many young women moved in with their boyfriends prior to marriage on a scale never before seen in history.[8]

The Baby Boomers brought up in the 1950's model of family life, wanted something not just different, but with equality between the partners. No longer were men the sole breadwinners while women stayed home with the kids. Unfortunately, the charts for navigating the intricacies of working out a successful relationship had not yet been updated. There needed to be something new, but we didn't quite know what that looked like. The models we were getting from our parents didn't fit our ideas of what happiness was all about. By the 1960's, there were so many fractured families that it was given a name, "The Generation Gap."[9] The close ties and strong traditions that had existed only a few generations ago had in many cases disappeared.[10]

Following the cultural upheaval of the sixties and seventies, the dynamics of relationships were permanently changed.[11] Could the conditioning of thousands of years of a patriarchal system be overcome? In the relatively recent past, over 240 years ago, the Constitution of the United States was written by and for white, male landowners. The continuing challenge is to reach equality and acceptance between men and women and respect for every person no matter their gender, economic situation, or culture as quickly and gracefully as possible.

During these turbulent times of the late 1960s, the Gay Liberation movement was also in its early stages of coming out from the shadows. Homosexuality was against the law and gays had to hide their sexual identity in the workplace and in the military. The majority of Lesbians, Gays, Bisexuals, Transgender, Queers, Intersexual and Asexual (LGBTQIA) were in the closet, living with the fear of retribution if they should be found out.[12]

To appear "normal" and avoid harassment, queer individuals were often in traditional heterosexual unions (Marriages of convenience in Hollywood during the 1920's were called "Lavender marriages").[13]

Gay marriage was not even a whispered possibility. Fortunately, there have been major strides in legislating civil rights for the LGBTQIA community, and we continue to move towards achieving equality.[14]

Although I am speaking from a heterosexual point of view, I have tried to make this book relevant for everyone.

You can create a meaningful union that will hold up throughout a lifetime, and achieve the loving partnership that you have always wanted. When you have the right tools and are willing to compromise and change, you can become the wonderful lover that your sweetheart is searching for.

When you evolve from being a single person into being in an intimate relationship, it's no longer just about you. Your partner's ideas of how s/he wants things, favorite activities, and dreams of the future all come into play. To get along, both of you have a responsibility to make the changes that will create a compatible life. That's a difficult thing to do and only some people are ready to do the work. Still, to keep your relationship current and to prevent issues from building up into something called "irreconcilable differences," there are the inevitable times when you have to get to the bottom of the disagreement. Most of the time you might think that whatever it is that is bothering you is not a big deal and you don't need to pursue it. Then, when you don't talk about it, this pesky little thing can blossom into a big deal.

This, what we called the "working-it-out" process, was one of the basic agreements of our intentional community known as The Farm in Summertown, Tennessee. In the early 1970's, during the back-to-the-land movement, 350 young people who had been meeting weekly for years in San Francisco, Ca. purchased 1000 acres in rural Lewis County, Tennessee. We considered our community a spiritual

> Most of the time you might think that whatever it is that is bothering you is not a big deal and you don't need to pursue it. Then, when you don't talk about it, this pesky little thing can blossom into a big deal.

school not unlike an ashram, only American hippie style. One of the basic tenets of our practice was to work on creating peace and happiness in the world. We knew that the only thing that we had control of was ourselves and if we modified the behaviors that got in the way of cooperative living, and worked on having harmonious relationships, there was a chance that we could raise the worldwide happiness quotient up a notch. We had an agreement among all the members of the community to discuss any problems that came up. We would give and receive feedback about our behaviors that were often beneath or sub to our conscious self, where many of our gremlins resided. The basic premise was that we have no idea about how we are perceived by others, but our unintended subconscious actions can cause negative reactions from family and friends. We also thought that by exposing the subconscious to the light of day, we gain understanding of our habits that block intimate relationships and keep change from happening. If a resolution couldn't be found, we would seek out help from friends in our community. In today's world, these "friends" are often psychiatrists, psychologists, or family counselors, but they can also be mentors who are in happy relationships. There were many nights when members of our multi-family household would sit around and "work it out." Not being trained in counseling or psychology, we learned by trial and error what helped and what escalated the dramas.

Creating an atmosphere of acceptance, trust, and compassion while talking about problems made it so our words didn't fall on deaf ears. Unfortunately, even with an agreement to change, resistance and animosity would still rear its ugly head and require patience, nonattachment, and unconditional love. This process was (and is) a difficult thing to do, to both listen and understand what your partner is trying to tell you, let alone making the necessary changes. When we made the choice to let down our defenses, knowing that the positive outcome would be good for both of us, a transformation took place that created a more peaceful household.

Although Robert and I were deeply in love with each other, at times our relationship was a nightmare and required huge amounts of work before we could find stability. When children arrived, the adventure became more challenging, since we wanted the best for our beautiful kids. The rewards for making those hard-won changes created a connection that allowed for the love to expand each time we came to an equitable agreement. Going through the process, within the crucible that was our school, trained us in a practice that has remained relevant throughout our forty-seven years of marriage.

There is an in-depth explanation on this subject in the chapters on Communication and The Subconscious.

I am not a marriage counselor, psychologist or licensed health-care professional. My credentials are borne out of a long, happy, continually evolving, and fulfilling marriage and the raising of our eight happy and successful adult children. These ideas are a guide to help you understand what was required for our relationship to work. When children are in the plan, we want to create a safe haven where the family can thrive. When we evolve compassionately and communicate graciously, we keep the love vibrant and passionate which is a foundation for a well-functioning family and a stable society.

Please contact the author on Facebook under Virginia Gleser, author, if you have a question or comment.

Love surrounds us always. It's just a matter of tapping into it.

Part 1. Marriage
Your Wedding Day

Congratulations! The unforgettable day of your wedding has arrived. No need to worry if it is not in perfect order down to the last table decoration. It is an amateur endeavor after all, and you have taken care of the important things and done your best. Your family and friends have gathered together to celebrate this special occasion and witness your affirmations of love and commitment. The bride, in all of her glory, makes her appearance and the groom proudly stands by her side. Emotions fly while you leave behind the single life. Everyone is focused and quiet while you say your vows and exchange rings. When the kissing stops, the ecstatic celebration begins with laughter, tears, toasting, and dancing with everyone giving their blessings as you begin your life-long journey together. These festivities will create memories that last a lifetime.

The synergy that exists in your union brings happiness and success, since the power of the two of you working together is greater than the sum of its parts. The life-long vows support the building blocks of agreements and compromise. A carefully constructed relationship will be your joint manifestation: a monument to your love, your values, and your commitment. When you nurture this union, it isn't just about you or your partner, but the intertwining of your two energies, your passions, your souls, your dreams, and your all encompassing love.

The Art of Marriage

A good marriage is created.

Within a marriage the little things are the big things.

It is never being too old to hold hands.

It is remembering to say " I love you" at least once each day.

It is never going to sleep angry.

It is having a mutual sense of values and common objectives.

It is standing together facing the world.

It is forming a circle of love that gathers in the whole family.

It is speaking words of appreciation and demonstrating gratitude in thoughtful ways.

It is having the capacity to forgive and forget.

It is giving each other an atmosphere in which each of you can grow.

It is a common search for the good and the beautiful.

It is not only marrying the right person,
It is being the right partner.

  -An anonymous poem that was hanging in my parents' home.

A Supportive Family and Community

Every wedding is unique, it doesn't matter if it is big or small, your family and friends with their collective experiences and perspectives come to celebrate your union and bring with them their love and support. Often, in modern ceremonies, the guests are reminded that they are witnesses to this marriage and hold a responsibility to be "the village" for the new couple when they are needed.

Traditionally, the community at large has been involved with the mentoring of married couples. The health of the household and the society depended on the childbearing couple's ability to be supportive and cooperative, and to bring up the next generation in nurturing and positive surroundings. A clan would not last long if it did not set guidelines learned through generations of trial and error. When the new partnership is launched and they have their freedom and independence as well as a support system to fall back on in times of stress or hardship, heartache is kept to a minimum and the community prospers.

Of course, there are plenty of couples that choose to elope or don't get married at all, but they also find it helpful to create a community around them. It wasn't too long ago that several generations lived close by in order to survive. Today, consider yourself fortunate if you can rely on a functional extended family. In our modern society, a support system can be difficult to find, especially when a job has taken you to a distant location. Creating your own social support network is the next best thing. Soon, you will have play dates for your children and someone to keep an eye on your house when you are away. From humble beginnings, your nuclear family can merge into a new community of friends and neighbors.

The Honeymoon

After the excitement of the wedding is over, you are now able to escape to a place where you can be alone, just the two of you. An exotic destination or somewhere special is the beginning of your married life, and you can finally unwind from the hectic schedule of the wedding.

Every couple has their own way of honeymooning. Robert and I had our marriage license signed by our minister, two witnesses, and the Justice of the Peace, whose office was in the gilded domed civic center in downtown San Francisco. The next day, we loaded up our 1942 Dodge school bus and set out on a journey across the U.S. Along with 300 like-minded friends we traveled with a caravan of 100 vehicles that sometimes stretched for twenty miles down the highway. Our trip continued on through the summer season when we arrived in Tennessee and settled onto our new land.

Although there are exceptions, think carefully before you invite friends, relatives and especially your parents to go along with you on your honeymoon. You already have more than enough of your parents within your psyche; you don't need to bring them along in person. A humorous movie a few years ago, (Sorry, I can't remember the title) portrayed newly-weds in bed having a spirited argument. Soon both sets of parents appeared next to their adult child helping them argue. It's Hollywood at its best, bringing the absurd reality into a visual picture. Whether you take a trip or keep it simple, this special time is for just the two of you. Bask in its uniqueness, this new beginning. It's a time when you can be together for the sole purpose of celebrating your love.

Now that you are married this new entity has a personality and integrity all its own. With your purest intentions, it will sparkle with unique artistry. It doesn't get any better than this.

The Art of Making Love

To keep the sparkling energy from the wedding and honeymoon alive for a lifetime, nourishing your love life is what keeps a vibrant relationship going. During intimate, sensual lovemaking with your sweetheart, you can feel the presence and connection to the universal life force, the closest thing to heaven on earth. You embrace the union of body, mind and spirit, a confirmation of your love. Celebrate the ecstasy!

The Eastern art of lovemaking, called Tantric Yoga, teaches that lovemaking extends to every minute of the day and night.[15] Your soft touch in the morning, and the first gentle things you say to each other, reaffirms your love. The passionate kiss good-bye punctuates an intermission until you relax again after a day's work. Joining in the kitchen to prepare dinner together, and telling each other about your day's events, stirs the joy of laughter and togetherness.

After a refreshing shower, you know what to do for your partner that will make him or her feel just right. If you run out of ideas, ask what s/he would like. There are books and videos of all kinds about lovemaking, but there is nothing more exciting than two people in love, exploring and discovering what turns each other on.

Tantric lovemaking is also about becoming "One." You are merging your astral, electronic, and physical fields. It's not long until your individual you-ness dissolves into a blending of the two of you. Both of you are unselfishly giving your all and receiving pure satisfaction in return.

Understanding the subtlety of a woman heightens your collective pleasure. When both of you take into account that women need a little longer to reach orgasm,[16] the guy can be gentle and patient and follow the woman's lead until you both achieve ecstasy. When you are pleasing her and taking the time to notice the subtleties of her body, you continue to move towards that perfect place. When you have mutual respect and trust for each other, it doesn't matter who is on top or who is steering. It becomes interchangeable.

If you can sneak in a "quickie" during a short break in your day, it's pure fun. It's a preview, a warm up to an extended leisurely time when you can bask in open-ended lovemaking, and feast on all of the gourmet courses and delicacies.

Occasionally, you will come home from work physically exhausted, or preoccupied, with your mind spinning off about this and that. How about a hot bath or a glass of wine? You begin to relax, let the day's worries and cares fall away, and when you reconnect with your lover it feels so good. After a massage, you might even fall asleep, only to continue where you left off in the morning, or the next evening, when you can be together again. Did the idea of coming home to your sweetheart keep you charged up all day at work? Hopefully, you weren't too distracted.

When you show each other how you want to be touched, you find each other's sweet spots. Slowly massaging your partner takes off the stresses and soreness of the day. Where are the places that hold tension that you can relieve with a rubdown? Is your touch too soft and tickly or is it too hard and deep? With practice, you can come to know your lover's body and be able to give him/her complete relaxation. Making love is about the whole experience not just the fireworks at the end.

Be creative; try new things and have fun. Your fantasies become a reality. Good sex happens when you are comfortable with your partner, safe and secure in each other's arms. A dynamic relationship develops when lovemaking is satisfying. Also, the deepest, most relaxed and healing sleep occurs after a sumptuous banquet of sex. It keeps tensions from building and can be the catalyst, the healing force, and the spirit that binds.

> **Thinking of you keeps me awake.**
> **Dreaming of you keeps me asleep.**
> **Being with you keeps me alive.**

The "One"

It has actually happened! You've found your true love! Do you feel like you've won the lottery? Are you walking on air? Before your sweetheart came into your life, did you go through a few previous relationships that for one reason or another didn't quite click? From these experiences, it became obvious what wouldn't work, and after narrowing down the essential qualities that you were looking for, you were lucky enough to find the perfect mate. Is s/he kind, tender, happy, intelligent, humorous, and fun? Did you have to make a few compromises because, after all, no one is perfect? Out of the billions of people on the planet, that wonderful someone with the basic qualities that you had in mind entered your life and everything is firing on all cylinders. The vision of a sweet home, maybe with children, and a life of adventure and happiness looks like it will bring you ever closer together.

The potential is there for "happily ever after," but as we all know, it is a thorny path. The question is: How do you keep the passion and romance alive? Can we agree that the perfect 'One' doesn't exist? Fortunately, love makes great things happen. The magical transformation appears when you want the best for each other. With mutual respect and persistence to forge new agreements to change, a frog will manifest into a prince and Cinderella into a princess. If the requisite characteristics for a wonderful lover are there, you can create your beautiful partner. S/he will grow into your expectations, and the rejuvenating power of love creates passion and beauty out of mere mortals.

Understanding how the Law of Attraction works is a fascinating phenomenon that might bring some clarity. Harville Hendrix in his books, *Keeping the Love You Find* and *Getting the Love You Want* writes poignantly about how who you are attracted to is "the composite of all of your caretakers,"[17] that is your parents, older sibling/s, and guardians. You have charmed your partner and s/he has enticed you in the same complicated web of love! Hendrix's basic premise is that the person that you are attracted to will have both the positive and negative aspects of the caretakers who raised you. So it is no wonder that this person, who looks like a prince or a princess one-day, may not feel like that the next! The exemplary qualities of you and your partner are the constant reminders of why you love each other, and the disagreeable qualities are where your challenges lie and what you will work on throughout your relationship.

Part of being in love is being able to change. Hopefully, along with your marriage vows, you have agreed to grow, change, and evolve. With the magic working, both of you will continue to be transformed into the beautiful "One."

> **"Being deeply loved by someone gives you strength,**
> **While loving someone deeply gives you courage."**   Lao-Tzu

After the Honeymoon

There is a common phenomenon that can occur following the sparkle of dating, the glow of the wedding, and the love fest of the honeymoon. In the comfortable atmosphere of unconditional love, you and your partner relax and reveal a little more of yourselves. It can come as a shock when all of a sudden, your *dirty laundry* (or who you really are) is scattered on the floor. The ecstasy of romance is sometimes blind to these habits, only seeing the purity of your soul, the openness of your heart, the sparkle in your eyes, and your 'highest self.' But now that the honeymoon is over, the blinders are removed and walls are exposed that have been built over a lifetime. You may see each other as you truly are with all your warts, farts, fears, and weirdnesses. It might even feel like the old 'bait and switch' routine. This isn't what I signed up for! Can you still love each other despite your human frailties?

Consider it a challenge to stay together and delve deeper into each other's worlds and let the intimacy grow. Unless current trends change significantly, a young couple marrying for the first time has a 50% chance of getting divorced within eight years. You have a better chance if you are over the age of 25 when you get married (those who do have a 24% less divorce rate), graduate from college (there is 13% less divorce), have children (40% lower than a couple without), or if your parents are happily married (14% drop in divorce). The odds improve if you don't fight about finances.[18] You would think that the love and ecstasy of a wedding would carry you farther, but the "happily ever after" ending in fairy tales is only the beginning of the journey. Eventually, (it happens to everyone) you run into seemingly irreconcilable differences. That is when an open compassionate channel of communication becomes one of the keys to a happy union.

For those who want to be seekers, the work brings great rewards. So, where do you start? How do you know what to talk about? Try saying what is on your mind and what you are feeling. Some of us are used to saying exactly what we feel, but often with an unfriendly tone that is hard to listen to and rarely brings about constructive change. In reality, most of us are uncomfortable exposing our deepest thoughts, and many of our feelings have been relegated to the basement of our psyche. But, when you actually connect with your partner and talk about what's on your mind, you will get in touch with your higher selves and then love can blossom.

Embrace your differences; you'll find that they add spice to your life. The challenge is to work through the hassles so peace can once again reign in the household. Doing this work creates that illusive magic that makes you Lucky in Love.

It might seem easier to avoid conflicts all together, than face that perilous trek into the psychic frontier and do battle with your collective demons. Why bother yourselves with this seemingly "Mission Impossible?" The answer is simply because working on change in your relationship makes for an exciting adventure. You always wondered if you could find true love and happiness and here is your big chance. Love, sex, and children thrive with an open, nurturing, evolving consciousness.

> **When I say, I love you more, I don't mean I love you more than you love me. I mean I love you more than the bad days ahead of us, I love you more than any fight we will ever have. I love you more than the distance between us, I love you more than any obstacle that could try and come between us. I love you the most.**

Are You a Good Partner?

How do you like being married? Have a few of the inevitable conflicts been easily resolved or do you sometimes become so embroiled that you wonder if this new arrangement is going to succeed? There is often a steep learning curve while your relationship begins to grow. Are you aware of what you are doing that contributes to the hassle? Do you wonder why you are even doing this? And then you remember that there is only one ever-elusive what-everyone-is-searching-for true love, and working through the problems and coming out the other side is what keeps a relationship vibrant and current.

Let's back up a little bit and try to understand the concept that you can only love someone as much as you love yourself. You were born into this world as a pure and wonderful being, and like a snowflake, perfect in your uniqueness. What you bring to the world is something that has never been here before, and your input will make a difference. And then your parents, teachers, and life experiences molded you. If your caretakers were kind, honest, supportive, and truthful, chances are that you have an authentic view of yourself. On the other hand, maybe your caretakers thought they were being kind, when they had no clue they were causing harm. You ended up with some habits that get you in trouble from time to time. Is your anger fuse too short? Are you stingy with your love? Are you unaccustomed to looking out for the needs of someone else? Changing unhealthy behavior is some of the work that is awaiting you. But for now, put your attention on all the positive and valuable qualities that make up who you are. If you are dedicated to finding true happiness, accepting and loving yourself right now is the first step.

While you continually try to discover how to

better care for your emotional, physical, intellectual, and spiritual needs, you can develop the qualities that make a great partner. To keep the love flowing, there are choices to make each moment of the day. Do you choose a healthy diet for your mind, body, and spirit? Can you appreciate periods of solitude? Do you spend time in nature? Can you visualize how powerful, intelligent, beautiful, imaginative, talented, and unique you truly are?

Self-love is about making the right choices. Soul-searching with the intent to make conscious changes to improve yourself is a lifelong endeavor. Do you allow yourself a second piece of cheesecake, or is it buying an expensive item that you can't really afford? Perhaps later when you find that you have added on a few pounds or run up your credit card bill, you realize that you can treat yourself better. Rewriting your script to make yourself into someone who you respect and admire will be an exciting challenge. There is only one person who is in charge of your future, and you can create yourself in any way that you desire.

Here's a great quote from Carolyn Myss's book, *Why People Don't Heal and How They Can*: "Regardless of what needs surface as you learn to know and love yourself, the important points are to give yourself the right of choice, self-expression, and self-respect."[19]

> **"Give yourself the right of choice, self expression and self-respect"**
> **Carolyn Myss**

Our Commitment is Tested

When Robert and I first met we were having a great time and arguments or hassles never came into the picture. However, as soon as we agreed to a committed relationship, issues seemed to pop up out of nowhere and a pleasant afternoon would turn into a nasty fight. What had happened to our easygoing ways of being with each other where nothing bothered us?

It seemed like the commitment to each other had opened up a door to allow our egos to relax, from trying to impress each other to transparently revealing who we really were. Even with our agreement to live on The Farm and follow the teachings of working out the subconscious, we had more than our share of ups and downs. At a particularly difficult time in our relationship, Robert moved out of our home for six months. We both needed to grow individually, and even with our agreement, and the support and encouragement of our friends, the actual transformation was way more difficult than we had imagined. Robert was committed intellectually to the idea of working things out, but was engulfed in old negative habits of anger, stubbornness, and disrespect that were especially directed towards me. I had to consciously work on keeping an attitude of unconditional love, and trust that he meant what he said about being open to change, when what I really felt like doing was throwing up my hands in disgust and forgetting the whole deal! However, with our many children, both of us knew that change was imperative and that if we didn't persevere with this deep soul searching that was required, we were on the brink of destroying the closely-knit family that we had worked so hard to build. When Robert returned, he knelt in front of me and gave me a wedding band to match his own, (something that we'd never had before) and begged me to take him back. He said he would do whatever was required to hold our relationship and family together. With our friends as witnesses, we reaffirmed our promises to change for each other. Although there would always be things to work through, this was proof that we could transform. Continually evolving through the years, this commitment has kept our relationship fresh, with vibrancy, love, and romance.

> When there is light in the soul,
> There is beauty in the person.
>
> When there is beauty in the person
> There is harmony in the home.
>
> When there is harmony in the home,
> There is honor in the nation.
>
> When there is honor in the nation,
> There is Peace in the world.
>
> From the Village Yoga Center in Modesto, Ca.

Tools for Creating the Love You Want

Whenever you take on a project, you accumulate a set of tools that helps make the job a success. It's no different in a relationship. Let's take a moment and tool up. Below is a guide to help you on your way to marital bliss. With a deeper understanding of how to become a good partner, you can find happiness.

The road you've chosen will be filled with beautiful scenery and exciting experiences. Inevitably, you will encounter potholes, breakdowns, and construction zones. Keeping these tools handy will help you deal with the "always somethings."

1. **Your positive attitude** affects the world around you. There are forks in the road where you have a choice to make the best of things as they are, or you can sink into being a complaining, grumpy curmudgeon. An optimistic approach to the hard times that life throws your way helps you find the blue sky peeking through the stormy clouds. It isn't only a cheerful face and kind words that makes up a positive attitude, but a heartfelt, turned-on feeling that emanates lightheartedness, honesty, integrity and sincerity. An appropriately cool bumper sticker says, **"Obstacles or Adventure, It's all in the Attitude."**

2. **Patience** is when you remain unruffled, in your "calm place," while the chaos, uncertainties, and fears of the world swirl around you. It is being tolerant with yourself and everyone else. You are working towards improvement and excellence, not perfection. There are times when your patience is put to the test when you deal with other people, but understand that they probably have their own issues that they are struggling with. A mellow perseverance will help you hold your course

while you make your way over life's hurdles.

3. **Flexibility** allows you to flow with whatever life throws your way. People, often out of fear or insecurity, become rigid in their thinking and want to have control over everything. Are you open to change? Of course, you want to let go of hurtful, stubborn, unyielding ways. Flexibility allows new creative ideas and concepts to grow, launching you into a higher state of consciousness.

4. **Acceptance** gives you the ability to appreciate yourself as you are, and in doing so, allows you to make the inevitable changes gracefully. Accept the present and then go forward into the new moment. Have you hit bottom? Uh, oh, made a mistake? Doing okay? Or living the Pura Vida? Whatever it is, embrace it as your starting point for the next adventure.

5. **Forgiveness** helps you accept and love yourself and everyone around you. Yes, we all have our faults and we've all made mistakes. Forgiveness forges a new path where you make amends and move forward, absolving yourself and everyone else of all the wrongs from the past. Every second is a chance for a new beginning. Putting hurts behind you can eliminate grudges and those feelings of revenge. Forgiveness bestows true freedom, unlocking the chain around your heart and opening it up to love and being loved in return.

6. **Non-attachment** is the knowledge and ability to deal with the fact that there are some things you cannot change. When you release that tight hold on something that is just not going to go your way, everyone wins. There are plenty of other possible directions to take, ways to be, things to do, and places to go. You can only change yourself; you can't change anyone else. You

cannot grab someone else's steering wheel and show them which way to go.

Serenity

Grant me the Serenity
To accept the things I cannot change,
Courage to change the things I can,
And wisdom to know the difference.[20]

7. **Tolerance**: Our planet is filled with a fascinating diversity of cultures, religions, and political systems. Unfortunately, mankind has this ridiculous, crazy-making tendency to want to look down on anyone who is different. Take your pick, black or white, women or men, poor or rich, immigrants, and so on. This way of thinking creates an "us versus them conflict." Biases and prejudices are usually handed down to you from your family and friends, and these teachings can be unlearned.

Seeing life from a different perspective challenges your ways of thinking and keeps you honest. Everyone who enters into your life has something to offer when you relate to him or her with kindness and respect. Sometimes being tolerant might mean accepting someone's wishes to be left alone. A lack of prejudice is one of the keystones for peace and understanding. If we can get in the habit of practicing it with each interaction, it can permeate the world.

8. **Gratitude** allows you to appreciate every experience or person that comes into your life. It's easy to be thankful for all the wonderful things that have happened, but when you are grateful for the difficulties and challenges that you have overcome, the reward

is self-confidence and empowerment. When you can transcend the beliefs that life is unfair, and that your frustrating troubles are someone else's fault, you can move on to living life to the fullest.

9. **Passion**: Whatever it is that brings fun and laughter into your life and inspires and excites you, that's where your passions reside. You might look back to the best of your childhood memories to find them. What did you love to do? What brought you the most happiness and feelings of fulfillment? When you pursue some of these things every day, whether it's taking a class, reading about it, looking it up on the Internet, or joining a group that is doing what you love to do, you'll start networking, hooking up, and coincidently finding yourself in a full-on, passionate lifestyle. Enjoying quality time with my family and friends, sailing, writing, dancing, living in nature, cooking, painting, giving and receiving massages, and listening to music are some of mine. What are yours?

The Subconscious

Many of our life-long habits, both positive and negative behaviors, have been learned from our parents or guardians, and the majority of these habits were instilled in us from a tender age and solidified through the years.[21]

Our annoying ways of being are not specifically designed to be provocative, but are rather subconscious, or unconscious, behavioral patterns. Since we are for the most part not aware of these mannerisms, there is little chance for us to make any changes. Unless someone puts a mirror up to our actions so we can see ourselves, these behaviors remain beneath our awareness, dwelling in our subconscious or even deeper in our unconscious. This section will delve into the intricacies of our psyches, and how we can overcome obstacles on the path to happiness and peace.

Disclaimer: The advice that is contained in this book is presented for informational purposes only. The material is in no way intended to replace professional medical care or attention by a qualified psychiatrist or a psychotherapist. If you find that you are disturbed or overwhelmed by anything about this subject, it might be prudent to seek professional counseling. In the event you use any of the information in this book for yourself, the author and the publisher assume no responsibility for your actions. This book cannot and should not be used as a basis for diagnosis or choice of treatment.

Allow me to digress a moment and discuss what the differences are between the conscious, subconscious, and the unconscious mind. R.J. Corsini and D. Wedding in *Current Psychotherapies*[22] distinguishes the three:

1. Conscious mind is "awareness in the present moment." We are conscious of what is happening around us.
2. Subconscious mind has access to information when you direct your attention to it. In the meantime it stays **sub** (under) your conscious mind. Once we have mastered skills like driving a car or riding a bike, speaking a language, or typing on a keyboard, they come naturally to us when we need them. If we do not use our abilities for a while, we may become a little rusty, but as soon as we use them again, they are there for us. Memories and ways of behavior can be accessed.
3. Unconscious mind sounds like you are medically out cold, but in psychological terms it is the part of the mind where we don't have easy access to the memories or information stored there. It includes childhood memories that we can't recall, and "beliefs, patterns and a subjective map of reality that drives our behaviors."

To keep it simple, I will use the word subconscious to include the subconscious and the unconscious. The practice that I'll be discussing is how to bring the subconscious to the surface by listening to feedback. Often we are oblivious to disruptive or unhealthy traits that are *sub* or beneath our conscious minds.

Most of these life-long habits have become our

automatic, spontaneous, default response to the world around us. From an early age, we often unknowingly indulge in anger, fear, shame, manipulation or running away to protect ourselves from harmful or fearful situations. In any couple's relationship, where intimacy is the embodiment of love, these behaviors create tension and distance. Once you become aware of your subconscious behavior, you are free to discard this "friend" that can sabotage you while you pursue a successful (happy) life.

When you begin to let go of the habitual reactions of moodiness, ranting, withdrawal, self-medicating addictions, or any other negative characteristic, you emerge out from the cocoon that has protected you from the complicated and sometimes stressful and hurtful world in which we live. The eventual result of releasing these negative energy habits is a lifting away of the blockage that prevented intimacy and communication from flowing freely. You will become empowered and courageous, prepared to explore the intricacies of your subconscious that challenge your happiness.

An open channel for communication is formed when you have a basic agreement with your partner that you can talk about things that are bothering you. This is a relatively simple agreement, but it has far reaching consequences. Breaking down the walls and barriers to unveil our subconscious to the light of consciousness releases amazing amounts of pent-up energy. The things that are troubling your partner about your behavior are subconscious to you and are hidden and prefer not to be

> **An open channel for communication is formed when you have a basic agreement with your partner that you can talk about things that are bothering you.**

revealed. However, when harmful or annoying habits are brought to your attention in a kind and compassionate manner, you become aware, and then can begin to work on letting them go.

When you explore the subconscious mind, there's a realization that certain patterns and belief systems have become obsolete and harmful. Studying their origins can determine how you want to change your crazy-making behavior. These embedded characteristics may have been a result of a scary or hurtful experience, or passed down to you through generations of your societal, cultural, or family conditioning. The idea is to do this work and melt the ice around your heart to free the love that's been squelched. When you bring to light your insecurities and fears, you are on your way to finding peace.

Listening to your partner is the only way you can gain an understanding of what is bothering him. Don't be surprised if he has to point out what you are doing numerous times. This is normal and gives both of you the chance to practice patience. It may take a while for you to see yourself through someone else's eyes, and then be convinced that it is necessary to make the effort to change a destructive habit.

To dredge up the muck in your emotional garbage dumpster is a touchy process. Often the tendency is to deny feedback, find excuses, counter-attack, or use other creative defensive mechanisms to keep from churning up the status quo. When your partner steps too close to your "stuff," there is a chance of raising such clouds of smoky confusion that he may forget what he was talking about. Do you make him feel like he is the problem for daring to bring it up? We all struggle at this point. The challenge is to just listen and not immediately get up your hackles and say, "No, no, no!" Can you understand what your partner is talking about? What is the content?

It is a time to be objective, while you refrain from fighting back. When you take a deep breath and let go, you may realize in your deepest soul that he is on to something. The challenge is to welcome the feedback and create new habits.

The ego wants to keep things as they are, and not rattle any cages.[23]   We all have walls built to protect us from real and imaginary threats, and only with trepidation would we want to tear them down and reveal our vulnerability. Who is this mate of mine? Can I trust him or her enough to let down my guard? Open up my heart and soul? Clear out the pain and leave myself unprotected and exposed? If your answer is "yes," it still takes courage, dedication, trust, and an open heart to say, "It is okay to go deep into those places because I have a partner who loves me enough to help me through it."

It's all about trust. What about the anger we feel when our trust has been violated? Did someone say they would do something for you, and then they didn't? Certainly, mothers occasionally run late picking up their children, and a kid may feel great pangs of abandonment thinking that his mother doesn't love him. Parents are not usually negligent or forgetful; they just run into unforeseen events like traffic snarls, or even naively think that a few minutes won't matter. These experiences helped create your early feelings of fear, mistrust, and neglect. Apparently, we all have certain events that mold our lives and flavor our actions.

> **It's all about trust.**

And then, there are the times when everything breaks down, and you blow it. Did your hair stand on end? Did your eyes take on that piercing glare, and your voice snap out ugly words? It becomes obvious that anger doesn't solve the problem, but rather escalates the situation. If you are serious about working on anger issues, perseverance and letting go can change your life.

When things start to go wrong, another thing that happens is to blame someone else for all of your problems. Wallowing around in a state of victimhood leaves you in turmoil that can adversely affect your physical, mental, and emotional wellbeing. You end up creating negative, energetic mischief that engulfs everyone in your vicinity with bad vibrations. How are you going to pull yourself out of this hole? How about letting go of the belief system that someone else can be in charge of whether you are happy or not. You are the creator of each moment, and no one can take that away from you. When you take a minute or ten to breathe in and breathe out, you can let go of this worn out belief system and acknowledge that you are in charge of your life.

You might take it a step further. How about apologizing to everyone who had to absorb your angry rages? Certainly it's a humbling experience, but it releases you from the drama and puts you back on the right track. If your sweetheart is a forgiving person and receives your apology, he might also accept his part in this situation and can return the favor. You may actually have created a common ground to talk about what came down and start building trust again. If things begin to change for the better, you might likely find out that he is what you thought all along, a wonderful person with integrity.

We are all reluctant to hear about our subconscious and being ready doesn't mean that we will be comfortable when we hear it. When you have the agreement to be each other's mirror into your inner workings, you will be able to discuss anything you want.

It makes a big difference when you ask your partner for permission to talk about a touchy subject. When you prepare yourself, checking to make sure there are no attitudes, anger, or frustrations, it's more likely that your partner will be receptive. You can't be attached to a person listening or changing. Sometimes, it is hard to stay gentle and patient with your partner while he works through something, but know that you will appreciate the same tender treatment when it's your turn to hear about your baggage.

There probably will be times when you just don't want to hear feedback and that's okay too. Even though you may have made an agreement to modify your behavior and work it through, there can be times when it feels overwhelming. It's fine to stop and give it a break.

The search for true happiness doesn't come without challenges and it takes courage to face your faults and weaknesses. When you can get over your fear of changing, and let go of these patterns, it frees you to find your authentic identity. When two people can work together on this on-going process, the end result is a happy union.

If you want to have a wonderful partner, be a wonderful partner. When you consistently make the effort to weed out unpleasant habits, your lover will be impressed and even more enamored by you.

> **In a stable and loving relationship, working it out and changing for each other becomes part of the routine. Issues are brought up and processed with respect. It doesn't mean that things don't sometimes get heated, but when the agreement is to work it through until you reach satisfaction, the ugly feelings disappear.**

Ten Steps to Illuminate the Subconscious

The following is a ten-step recipe for bringing the subconscious into consciousness. This practice can help a relationship evolve into a loving and intimate partnership, while going through a challenging metamorphosis. These steps build a foundation on which your love can deepen, mature, and maintain its vibrancy and romance.

1. Make an Agreement with your partner that it's okay to tell each other about bothersome subconscious habits. To open a discussion, agree to ask permission to see if this is a good time to talk about something.

2. Begin by saying how much you love each other. Remain compassionate, kind, and patient, with a large dose of humor and unconditional love.

3. Listen respectfully to what your partner has to say. Try to understand what she is saying about your behavior. Your partner has been courageous enough to bring up something that she knows will be difficult for you to hear. Resist the ego's urge to make excuses, lash back in anger, walk out, or put it back on your partner. She is not your enemy, but your lover and the messenger. She is carrying good news, liberating news. When little and big issues are taken care of, and each of you has listened and agreed to work on changing for yourself and your partner, the relationship sparkles.

4. Continue your commitment to work on changing the habit. Notice the breakthrough that happens when you become aware of what your partner is trying to tell you while you are in the middle of doing it.

5. Laugh at yourself when you are caught in the act. Stopping in mid-stream to enjoy the process means you are on your way towards a happier self.

6. Recognize and revisit the events, beliefs, and teachings of your past that caused you to adopt this unhealthy behavior, and acknowledge that you don't need it any longer. When you arrive at the realization that you don't need this toxic "friend," you will understand how your old crusty habits may have made it difficult for you to be in a satisfying, intimate relationship.

7. Release old patterns and experiences: a radical shift that takes place deep within your body, your mind, and your emotional self, even down to your DNA. Every cell moves over to accept the change. Waves of light and energy flow within and around you, relieving you of the burdensome weight that you have unknowingly been carrying around for so long.

8. Forgive yourself, and make the change deep within out of love and respect for yourself and your partner. Move forward on the path that will attract happiness and freedom.

9. Stay vigilant. There is always the possibility that over time, in a stressed out moment, you might revert back to your old comfortable ways, the former default setting. Your loving and patient partner can then gently remind you to continue your practice.

10. Resentment can show up when you don't talk about your partner's negative behavior that bothers you. Frustration can grow when you bravely bring something up and your partner doesn't want to hear

it and then gives you a hard time. Is there sufficient trust in the relationship to believe that what you are asking him or her to change or modify will actually improve your lives together? When stubbornness is overcome, and there is courage to change, you both can find peace of mind.

A negative behavior pattern can often feel like a comfortable old friend who unfortunately is no longer an appropriate or healthy influence. There is a tendency (everybody does it) to fight change and dig in your heels. There are all sorts of ways to rationalize holding onto your old ways, going so far as to lash out in anger, come up with outlandish excuses, and run away, denying that you ever wanted to change in the first place.

But your higher self knows better and can triumph. When this happens, you Let It Go, Let It Go, Let It Go. This amazing release brings tears of joy to replace the tears of desperation, anger, and self-pity. Emotionally cleansed, you feel lighter and happier. You feel both confidence and humility, mixed with joy and thankfulness.

This process is one of the hardest things that you may ever do, but when you are willing to create the new you, it brings the biggest payoff, infinite love and happiness.

‖ Let It Go, Let It Go, Let It Go

Communication

When the communication doesn't flow, the relationship struggles along trying to bridge the ever-widening gap of solitude that prevents knowing what each other needs and wants. Researchers Drs. Robert Levenson, John Gottman and Howard Markman, working at the University of California, Berkeley and more recently at the University of Washington, explored the ways that couples argue and fight.[24] By observing how the partners communicated, they were able to predict with amazing accuracy the relationships that had a good chance of surviving and which ones would fall apart. The scientists found that the most destructive behavior for a marriage was contempt and criticism, followed by stonewalling and defensiveness. Hoping to minimize this behavior, they introduced a set of simple ground rules for peaceful and productive communication based on Robert's (not my guy) Rules of Order.[25]

They discovered that this orderly format could restore reason and civility to any necessary discussion when the situation has deteriorated to a contentious mess. These guidelines may seem rigid, stiff, or too formal, but if you customize them to your own taste and then use them on a regular basis, they can become a lifeline by which you and your partner can pull yourselves out of the abyss.

An Updated Robert's Rules of Order

1. Only one person speaks at a time.
2. The person speaking states the problem while the other listens.
3. The listener shows that s/he understands by stating the problem in his or her own words.
4. The person who originally brought up the problem confirms that the listener has grasped the issue correctly.
5. The original speaker states how he or she would like the problem solved.
6. The listener makes concessions and agreements.
7. If there is another side to the issue, the same rules apply, but first the original speaker receives satisfaction.
8. If anyone has felt offended or mistreated, a sincere apology, tenderness, and forgiveness can clear the air.

In addition to these guidelines, the following chapters provide suggestions to help you and your partner create the mood for considerate communication.

Tools for Your Communication Toolbox

TIMING is Everything. Resentments start to creep in and multiply when something is bothering you and you don't talk about it. Ideally, it's best to address the issue when it happens. But if you have missed the opportunity to say something at the time, you still deserve satisfaction. If you worry that this issue will cause trouble, or is trivial, or it would be better to just forget about it, this is probably an indication that you still need to talk it out.

When your partner first walks through the door after a long stressful day at work give him/her time to relax before bringing up the problem. The situation has a better chance of working out successfully with fewer explosions, when you wait until after a shower and a nice dinner. Realizing that there is a source of irritation itching to burst out and ruin the mood, take ten deep breaths (releasing any anger or irritation while envisioning a successful discussion) and then gently and compassionately ask if you can talk to him or her about something. Leave plenty of time to sort things out. After all, your job is relatively easy compared to the hard work s/he has of listening, receiving, and changing.

Making a habit of sorting out disagreements when they first pop up prevents issues from accumulating down the road. The alternative is to stuff it down in some hidden place where it ferments and builds to a pressurized outburst. Unresolved hassles do not vanish, but devour the love.

ASKING PERMISSION. When our kids were young, there were times when Robert and I needed to talk to them about unacceptable behavior. We expected them to listen with respect and develop new habits for themselves. We understood that our children were our mirrors, and when the dust settled and we had time to reflect on what was happening, their negative behaviors were more often than not a direct reflection or reaction to the way we were. When we altered our course, it was easier for them. Like all children, perhaps they were also simply testing us to understand the limits of the family boundaries.

Then, in a relatively short time, the children grew into adults, and one fine day our daughter requested that we please ask her permission before we gave out advice. At first we were surprised since aren't we the parents who get to say whatever we want? But she was right and when we embraced the concept, it turned out to be a healthy step that among other things changed the parent/child relationship into an adult/adult friendship. It was a reasonable request, which led to a more trusting and respectful dialogue. Our other adult children appreciated the change too, and the discussions between us became more receptive and easy going. We thought it was a good idea to ask permission in our own relationship as well, eliminating a whole level of confusion, negativity, and chaos when we dealt with touchy issues. It also prompted us to take it a step farther. We wanted to define what this request for permission meant. We called it "The Contract."

"**THE CONTRACT.**" Before you begin these often-loaded conversations, **ask your partner if this is a good time to discuss a problem**. If she agrees, then continue. By giving her permission, she feels that you are not in "attack mode" and the conversation can smoothly continue. Of course, she may answer, "Uh oh, what is it now?" But when you make this process a habit, trust builds. While the answer still might be "Uh, oh," when she acknowledges that it is for the best, she may also say something like, "Okay, what do you have for me?"

Both of you have displayed courage, you to bring up this uncomfortable issue, and your partner for agreeing to hear what you have to say. If your partner isn't ready or asks you to change your tone, she may want to choose a more opportune moment. With your mellowed attitude, for instance, it is likely that she will then have a more receptive ear. A consistent refusal to sit down and talk about things could be a deal breaker and a "red flag." Without communication, the relationship is heading for a breakup or perhaps worse, a debilitating, stagnant life of mediocrity. A common complaint from married couples is that the spark has been doused, like B. B. King sings in "The Thrill is Gone." "Where is the exciting lovemaking we used to have? We just come home, eat, watch TV and go to bed when we used to talk for hours about everything." When either of you is not willing to discuss what's on your mind, the love, respect, and trust drains out of the relationship.

When you do not discuss the issues, you allow the garbage of unresolved conflicts to collect. The pile can grow so high that sooner or later a couple may split up, insisting that there is too much stinky refuse to deal with. The legal terminology for this mess is "irreconcilable differences." Changing partners usually doesn't help if you haven't embraced your feedback and evolved. You are still who you are, and the garbage will just start to collect again. Dumping the trash on a regular basis and working through the changes is routine maintenance, essential to long-term happiness.

Below are guidelines for making "The Contract," and steps you can take when you ask your partner permission to talk about something that is bothering you.

Take a moment to relax and find that calm place within. Scan yourself, making sure you are in a kind, forgiving, and unconditionally loving frame of mind.

1. And then ask, "Can I talk to you about something?"

2. "What I am about to tell you will be helpful to us both, and it is necessary for our wellbeing. I will say it nicely and with respect."

3. "It takes bravery to bring this issue up, and more courage for you to hear and receive the message gracefully."

4. "Please listen respectfully and consider what I have to say. I would like a full agreement, but a "maybe" is satisfactory. A "no" is unacceptable. A "no" response indicates that you do not trust my viewpoint enough to consider that what I am saying has merit. A "maybe, I will consider it," is not what I prefer but is an adequate response.

5. "You can call off this discussion at any time, with the understanding that it will be continued later."

6. Please note: If someone gives permission reluctantly, feeling like they are being pressured, or says "Okay," without sincerity, you should stop. Without them on board, inevitably, the situation will deteriorate into an angry, frustrating quarrel and rarely can any progress be made. **Your message is not going to get through. Ask if there is another time to talk when he or she will be more receptive. You cannot be attached to someone else's enlightenment.**

MAYBE IS OKAY. When your partner brings up an issue, he clearly knows what his concerns are. Hopefully, you will listen to the whole story without interruption. He might not have all of the correct facts, and he probably is adding his own fears and subconscious attitudes to the situation, but that's not the point. **Try not to have your first response be an argumentative "No."** Or do you say "I didn't do that," "You don't know what you are talking about," "You have it all wrong, I totally disagree," or do you put it back onto your partner and say that it is "all his fault?" These are all defenses that prevent changes from happening. Perhaps instead of these retorts, you can anticipate the inclination to say "No," pause for a moment and contemplate what he is saying. At least give him a "Maybe, I will consider it," or "I will think about it." Your partner would prefer a "Yes, you are right," but a "Maybe" is so much better than a "No, you are wrong, I didn't do that." Wouldn't it be earth-shaking if you could say, "I understand what you are talking about; it rings true, and I will work on changing it?" Ideally, you will realize that your partner has a valid point, and you can give him or her satisfaction by appreciating what he is talking about.

Once we had made this agreement we were amazed at how responsive each of us was to what the other had to say. There was also the added bonus that when Robert wanted to tell me something and asked permission with that tone of annoyance and irritation, I could ask him to take a chill pill, and ask me again later. When he cut loose of his uptight attitude, the message was easier for me to hear. Asking permission relieved the stacked, tense feeling, and talking about it could then begin on a relaxed footing.

HUMOR. Laughter chases the blues away, and a light-hearted touch eases the challenge of making changes. Even when things seem terribly serious, a humorous remark or a smile of recognition can make the workout easier to stomach. When you have plowed through the muck, anger, and pain, and understand what your partner is trying to say, it becomes an occasion for celebration. Laughing at yourself is a sign of maturity as well as making you fun to be with. Your humor makes light of the seemingly mystifying, ugly, and sometimes, scary monsters that hide in the depths of your psyche. When you do not take yourself so seriously, it's easier to let go of grouchy and stubborn attitudes, and they evaporate into thin air.

Humor is an art worth cultivating, especially when you can laugh at yourself. It is those humbling moments when you realize you've been an ass that can allow an uncomfortable situation to dissolve into laughter.

THE TALKING STICK. When you constantly interrupt each other, communications disintegrate into an unpleasant shouting match. The person speaking should have the respect of the listener. It is a custom in some Native American meetings and ceremonies to have some valued object like a stick, pipe, or feather that is passed around the circle to each person who has something to say. It is understood that the person holding the "talking stick" can speak without interruption and be given undivided attention. The speaker then passes it to her partner, and then he also receives the same courtesy. As the discussion proceeds, each of you has the time and space to complete your thoughts.[26]

Is there an object, which you could use for this purpose that holds special value to both of you?

TAKE TURNS. Taking turns is one of those things that we hopefully learned in kindergarten, and when it comes to communication, you respectfully take turns listening to each other's points of view.

Let us suppose your partner has built up her nerve to bring up a topic that is bothering her, something that she would like you to change. Is she worried that you will become stubborn and come back with a barrage of excuses? When one person comes up with enough backbone to open up a possibly explosive discussion, there is a tendency for the other partner to see this as an opportunity to unload his pent-up issues. This is your partner's turn, and you need to be sensitive by genuinely listening. Of course, there are other sides to the issue or maybe other issues. However, you may have to wait for another day to discuss your gripes. Eventually, there will be time for you to have your say, but only after your partner feels that there has been a satisfactory resolution to what was on her mind. If you can gracefully receive the information about yourself, maybe when it is your partner's turn to listen to you, she will reciprocate in kind.

TAKE A FEW BREATHS OR TEN. To make sure that you are not "uptight" when bringing up a subject, it helps if you check yourself and take a few deep breaths. While you're breathing, you can meditate for a minute and create a mindset that is expansive, compassionate, unattached, and gentle. Then, in the kindest way possible, tell her what is on your mind and more than likely she will sense your good intention. It also helps to find your calm place when your partner asks you if she can talk to you about something. It creates a relaxed and receptive mood that makes it easier to listen and let things go.

The recipe is simple enough: Trust that you love each other, speak the truth, fear no one, be kind, even humorous, and hold your temper.

LISTENING. Being a good listener is essential for respectful communications. It's so easy to talk on top of each other, thinking you have something more important to say. Do you jump into those pregnant pauses, not allowing your partner to stop and formulate his thoughts, and interrupt or finish the sentence for him? How about even if your partner isn't totally perfect in his delivery, can you slow down enough to understand and grasp the content of what he is saying and make closure with that? Taking offense at his attitude or lack of confidence makes it harder to listen to what he is trying to say. Becoming defensive during discussions also squelches your understanding of your partner's perspective, and you hear only what you want to hear. When you take it personally and become upset, feeling like you have been attacked, minimized, and victimized, your reaction is likely to be one of resistance and denial. Inevitably you then miss the crucial point that your partner is trying to make. If you can mellow out and drop your defenses, remembering that the love of your life is trying to break through your stale habits, you can listen when she says her "peace."

GIVING AND RECEIVING. In a normal conversation, communication flows easily back and forth. Even when a discussion meanders and goes on detours and tangents, both of you can feel included, knowing that in the end you will both be heard.

However, when someone is always giving and the other partner is always receiving, it's a one-way street. One person will feel resentment, and animosity will grow while the relationship is diminished interaction by interaction. There is the story about the passing of the gold coins, for instance, that our mentor, Stephen Gaskin, liked to tell. Two friends pass a gold coin back and forth. If one of them is stingy or selfish, he will shave a few slivers off of the coin and pass it back, accumulating a small pile of ill-gotten gains. Eventually, his friend will feel short-changed since he didn't receive an equal share, and the friendship inevitably erodes away. When the two-way street of give and take is open, communication is on track and you can easily talk about anything.

SATISFACTION. When your partner tries to bring up a touchy subject, there is often a tendency to counterattack. This is an offense used as a defense, with two people pointing fingers at each other and never connecting. Let's say, for example, that your partner brings up the time when you went on that shopping spree. He says that you are not living within the budget while racking up ridiculous interest on your credit cards. Without acknowledging what he said, you reply that he never takes you out anymore and, besides, he is stingy. One problem is now layered on top of another.

Your partner probably agonized all day over how to bring up this sensitive subject of finances. Why not give him a little respect for having the nerve to talk about your overspending? Do you realize that you are slightly out of control about this? Can you resolve the initial issue to his satisfaction before introducing another problem? Just because your partner opened the gates of a discussion, does not mean you can flood the conversation with your agenda. You may need to look into what prompts you to spend too much. It's responsible economics to stay within the budget and pay down debt, leaving you with a set amount of expendable cash for each month. When you resolve the credit card issue to your partner's satisfaction, perhaps he will not be so worried about finances and will feel like taking you out for a night on the town.

RECEIVING FEEDBACK GRACEFULLY. It takes courage to hear what she wants to tell you, and it feels so good when you receive it gracefully and agree to process the baggage. Imagine touring New York City on a beautiful clear day, and you are taking the elevator towards the 102nd floor of the Empire State Building where you will have that famous, expansive view. On the way up, when the elevator stops at the third floor, you wouldn't think of getting off. Why would you leave the relationship stranded at a boring level rather than follow it to its highest potential?

APOLOGIES. Apologies and forgiveness clears the air. Trust, respect, love, and even repairing friendships are possible. There's an understanding that you've done something that you regret, and you want the situation to improve. It's an opportunity to make things better for you, your partner and your family. Apologizing is the initial step of giving up the energy that your unkindness has snatched away. Making a sincere apology may be one of the hardest things you'll ever do, but it begins to turn an unhappy situation around for the better.

If your partner has made a valid point in the heat of an argument, saying "You are right about that," and "I am sorry," can alleviate the tension. It's normal to feel vulnerable when you admit that you were wrong or that there is something you need to change, but when you apologize it opens up your heart.

Women and men have a different approach to apologies according to two studies done at the University of Waterloo in Ontario, Canada. Elizabeth Bernstein writes that it might seem that women apologize more than men, but according to the study, both men and women apologized about the same amount. It came as a surprise that people apologized more to their friends (46%) than to their romantic partners (11%), and more to strangers (22%) than to their family members (7%). Men tend to worry that an apology lowers their standing with their peers and is not beneficial in a competitive business setting. Women often use an apology to smooth out a rough spot in a friendship or to empathize with someone like, "I'm sorry you've had a tough time,"[27] rather than to admit that they have done something wrong. But when an apology is an admission of a mistake and a promise to do better, it becomes a valiant and even heroic step of taking responsibility for your actions with the intention to make amends. To continue on and complete the metamorphosis that leads to reconciliation is the real test, but a heartfelt apology can be the start of a liberating transformation.

Unfortunately, there are people who just can't seem to admit that they are wrong and since they are never wrong, they don't need to apologize.[28] When one of you says, "This is who I am, you can't ask me to change anything," is this The Popeye Syndrome, "I yam what I yam?" If this sounds familiar, at the very least the partnership will lose its vitality. Is it worth being so stubborn that you jeopardize this relationship? Many couples that have separated can go back and remember exactly when one or both partners dug in their heels. Did one of them challenge the status quo and insist on change, while the other person refused to budge? When you realize how much time, work, and emotional energy you have invested in your relationship, the decision to adapt is obvious. Remember why you picked this person out of the crowd, out of all the many people that you dated? What made him or her so special? Didn't you think s/he was the best companion possible? Weren't you so in love?

CHANGE. In order to keep a relationship flourishing, it needs to continually evolve. When you have been asked to change something by your partner, the essence of who you are is not on the chopping block and neither is your style, your sense of humor, or your personality.

A certain amount of discipline is required to eliminate long-standing habits that sabotage happiness. For instance, when two people are communicating and one of you is being selfish, not wanting to hear it, getting angry, or being rude, the other person is insulted, resentment builds, and the love is whittled away.

Often the hassles become so intense that the "grass seems greener on the other side" syndrome sets in. People separate and decide to try their luck with a new partner. If you are not in the habit of working things out and evolving, eventually your new partner will confront the same issues since you are still you. These habits remain no matter whom you are with. Serial monogamy does nothing to chase the gremlins out of your subconscious. They do not disappear until you consciously usher them out of your life. If you can make an agreement to work things out, you can **"love the one you're with."**[29]

The part of you that is difficult to be with is behavior you can change. These annoying, divisive, unhealthy, and harmful habits can include anger, arrogance, unkindness, envy, stubbornness, aloofness, and defensiveness, to name but a few. If you refuse to modify your actions, you can end up in a lonely, grouchy rut, whereas changing your habits carries you to a higher level.

SURRENDER. It takes monumental courage to allow a transformation to happen. Do you know what it feels like to totally surrender? It's a healthy exercise to find that quiet, safe place deep within, let it all go, and feel free and unencumbered. Practicing with your partner is the true test. When you find yourself in a situation that you've talked about, it helps to focus your intention to change with a mantra such as, "Relax, relax, or let go, let go, or zip it, zip it" ("Zip it" is keeping your mouth shut when your tendency is to say something snippy or unkind that only makes the situation worse). Loosening up enough to "let go" may make you feel defenseless, exposed, weak, or frightened. Letting go of pride and stubbornness may appear to threaten your very essence, and yet to surrender empowers your warmhearted self to emerge.

Like plaque blocking an artery that brings on a heart attack, stubbornness, pride, anger, and fear block the joy, sweetness, and happiness from our lives. And then when your heart is finally opened, immediately you are vulnerable. Take a step towards intimacy and, inevitably, there is the possibility of pain. He's your sweetheart, and yet he's bringing up issues that have been comfortably repressed and tucked away. He is exposing them to the light of day, and it is no doubt distressing. A successful relationship requires 100% commitment from both partners; it's all or nothing. Only by letting go and allowing the walls to come tumbling down can you unblock the flow of love. You will be loved in return.

TIMEOUTS. This process of working things out comes with a warning. Your partner may have given you permission to talk about an issue, but when it was presented ever so nicely by you, for some reason or other, he refused to hear it. It was too painful or embarrassing, bringing up such a deep hurt, or challenging his pride, or the very nature of who he thinks he is. Was his first impulse to "kill the messenger?" But, the issue hasn't gone away, and you still have to deal with the problem and try to make it better.

How about a fifteen-minute timeout or the proverbial walk around the block? The situation can become so heated that you need to disengage and take a break, with the understanding that the discussion is simply being placed on hold. You are not going to forget about it and neither should he. Let the issue sleep while the "cease-fire" is in progress. When cooler heads prevail, come back and pick it up again. There is a tendency to avoid **getting back into it,** but if you let things slide, they will return to haunt you. Going to bed with an unresolved hassle is a no-no! This is different from "bagging it" because you are going to try to continue working it out after a break.

BAG IT. If progress is stalled, you can agree to disagree. After everything is said and done, and there is still a disagreement consider "bagging it." That is:
1. State the problem clearly.
2. Tie it up neatly and agree to bring it up again with a trusted third party.
3. You then have the luxury to forget about it. There is no reason to tear up a relationship over one issue. Outside help is available when you need it.

Sometimes while mulling over what transpired, a new perspective sheds light on the subject, and the **big** person comes to an understanding that his/her partner has a point. If this realization should come to you, don't hesitate to admit that she was right. Perhaps this was the missing piece in the first place, and things can then work out easily. You may not need that third opinion, and you can realize how your acknowledgment and/or apology can re-energize the discussion and make way for an equitable conclusion. It takes **two to tango** and, after taking time to reflect on the issue at hand, both of you may gain insights that clear the way for new agreements.

THE FAIR WITNESS. When you cannot reach satisfaction on an issue, the two of you can take it up with a trusted third party, which is a lot better than bringing it to a divorce court. A fair witness can be a diplomatic friend, a happily married person or couple, or a relationship counselor who you both feel comfortable with. The friendly referee, who is obviously not emotionally involved in the argument and may have seen it many times before, usually has a clear understanding of the problem. This person brings a fresh perspective and can help you work things through to a successful conclusion. An impartial viewpoint is simply a mirror held up for you to see things clearly.

Are there issues that you have decided to leave unchallenged, the dangerous "shared subconscious" that leads to enabling each other's destructive behaviors? A mentor can also help you through these difficulties that are common in everyone's life. Another person's viewpoint can give you objectivity and a refreshing new way to deal with your problems.

NEGATIVE ENERGY HABITS. Imagine that you are a bucket full of water and that arguing, complaining, angry words, stubbornness, and being grouchy are holes in your bucket where your energy drains out, sapping the health and vitality from your relationship. The only way to patch up these holes is by letting go of these negative energy habits. Having a full energy bucket alters the whole dynamic, bringing love back into your life.

It's easy to become caught up in a toxic drama when you react to your partner in the same old predictable way. Around and around the negative vibrations go like a "loop." Every time this pattern comes up, the same scenario unfolds. The tendency is to want **the other person** to change. **The secret to ending a 'loop' is changing what *you* are doing and refraining from your habitual response when the loop comes 'round again.** When you change, the loop collapses, frustrations subside, and healing takes place. This allows a door to open making it easier to deal with the real issues that the loop was about in the first place.

BE KIND. Most of us indulge ourselves with rationalizations of why we can be angry, crabby, accusatory, shaming, or unkind. We come up with the excuse that we can be this way because of what our partner did, or due to a situation outside of our control. You might feel frustrated and feel that you have a right to take it out on someone else, and the closest target is often your sweet companion, the love of your life. There is a certain comfort zone in this ugliness. These reactions then become normal behavior, which leaves you drained by the end of the day. You can make an agreement with your partner that **there is no reason to be nasty, despite any offense.** An angry attack, a tirade, sarcasm, or any unkindness only creates resistance and resentment instead of the positive results you are seeking. The cure can be taken from a page in the kindergarten manual; be nice, be kind, and share. Amidst all the dust and smoke, jumping down off of your high horse can also clear the air and allow you to move forward.

Karma and Personal Responsibility

Understanding the concepts of Karma can help you take charge of your life. Karma is an Eastern term that has embedded itself into the vernacular and is loosely translated as: "For every action, there is a reaction." Common sayings about this universal law include, "what goes around, comes around," and "as you sow, so shall you reap." Karma can also be translated as "Luck" or "Fate." Another way of looking at it is whatever situation you find yourself in now is due to choices you have made in the past. You might ask, "How could I have chosen such a terrible life?" Are you tempted to be angry at the universe, at God, your parents, or yourself? Is somebody else the reason for your unpleasant situation? If you don't like where you are, make better choices in the present. This seemingly awful life can be looked on as a teacher that you have chosen, an instructor who leads you to your passion, your purpose, and true happiness. How you live your life each and every moment is the practice. **You have to start somewhere and that might as well be right here and right now.** Soon enough, you will discover if what you are doing is the right path. You always have the power to make adjustments as you go along.

Every moment there are choices to be made. You can learn from your mistakes or count on repeating them again and again. Life is that great teacher that won't let you slack off without consequences. Maybe when you have tripped up one too many times, you will have a realization that you need to watch where you are going, and live each day with awareness and personal responsibility.

Every moment there are choices to be made. You can learn from your mistakes or count on repeating them again and again. Life is that great teacher that won't let you slack off without consequences…live each day with awareness and personal responsibility.

You have to start somewhere and that might as well be right here and right now.

"Wholeness is not achieved by cutting off a portion of one's being, but by integration of the contraries."   Carl Jung

Feedback

When you are on an angry tirade, you'd be shocked to see a video of yourself. You can't imagine that you look that disgusting, and you'd never let anyone talk to your sweetheart that way!

Constructive feedback, a compassionate appraisal, can let you know how you appear and how your actions affect those around you. When you acknowledge what you are doing and begin steps to amend your behavior, you'll avoid being that clueless person who wonders why their partner just up and left.

Most people's first reaction to feedback might be to feel hurt or insulted, as if it is a stab to their self-esteem, and what they consider to be their very essence. Yet with reflection and time to evaluate what your love is saying, you realize that a valuable, hidden part of you is being uncovered. When light is shed on one of your negative qualities and you feel uncomfortable, maybe even angry, off-balanced, and embarrassed, it is possible through all the smoke to understand at least an inkling of what she is talking about. You may even realize that, "I've heard that somewhere before." Being open to feedback is never easy, but if you can pause for a moment to look at it objectively, you will agree that these valuable changes can make your life better. You might say, "Bring it on! What do I have to lose, a dysfunctional, crazy-making ego?"[30] Life generally gets sweeter when you dump the garbage.

When you cultivate the skill of listening to your feedback, a transformation can happen. Sharpening your discerning skills will allow you to see what other people are saying and whether their feedback is right for you. You can recognize the love in your partner because she is the one who appreciates you despite your flaws. No one says it's easy to hear what is being said, but she is trying to tell you the truth about yourself, and does have your best interests at heart, doesn't she? Your first impulse, like most of us, is to fight back, argue, put up smoke screens, walk away, bring up all sorts of excuses, or defend yourself. It doesn't hurt to take a break at this point because after all, you can't hear anything in that agitated state.

When you are ready to be receptive, understand that your best friend is trying to help by giving you her perspective. It may not necessarily be something you think you need or want to change, but it is certainly worth your time to listen and consider the feedback. Can you, without being paranoid, evaluate where she is coming from and what her motives might be? If that all checks out, can you add her suggestion to your to-do list, something that you work on for your own good? Resist the temptation to say, "No, I don't do that! Leave me alone." When you consider what is being said, can you say, "Maybe there's some truth to that? I'll consider it." A "Yes, I know what you're talking about, and Thanks" would be a welcomed response.

Is there a tendency to insist that you are always right? Let's suppose your partner tells you that your deodorant isn't doing its job. Do you feel humiliated? Consider your sweetheart's point of view. She is the one who has to live with you after all. What is the big deal if you take more showers or change your clothes more often?

Or how about something heavy like when she is brave enough to mention that your temper is out of hand; do you feel your anger wanting to burst out? What can you do to diffuse the situation without blowing your top? Learning to handle anger is a difficult thing to do, but you'll find your life changes for the better when you make the effort to stay cool when your hair stands on end. Anger can be a positive emotional response to injustice, intolerance, and mistreatment. How you channel that rage into positive results can make things better for everyone. You want to be able to talk about your feelings and about the things that well up inside of you, without ranting, throwing things, or hurting yourself and others.

Accepting feedback requires that you make a commitment to change. The practice of being open to hearing what your partner is saying is cultivated throughout your lifetime. Having decided to walk down a path to a happy life, and agreed that you have changes to make, there are still times when it seems like this practice is requiring too much. Maybe you want to go back into your old shell and be the way you've always been: rage at the world and refuse to listen to your partner. Okay, but how does keeping all that negativity in your life make you feel? When you look at all the changes you have already made and the new opportunities that have come your way, before long you'll be ready to take another leg of your journey towards a higher consciousness. We all lose our way from time to time and that is what makes us human. But even the detours can turn out to be our teachers, so not to worry.

It's a personal growth opportunity when you make the choice to alter your negative habits. Your partner will surely appreciate it. You might ever so kindly and gracefully, try some day to give her feedback too. Will she follow your example? When you evolve with one another, your love strengthens.

> "True love has no expiration date."
> Artist Carl Larsson

Uh, Oh, Negative Habits

Here are seven positive actions that you can take to clear out negative habits:

Step One: What would you like to change? Accept that this behavior is a part of you. In yoga when you have pain, you breathe into that pain, feel it, and stretch in different ways to enhance or relieve the discomfort. When you begin to understand the way the muscles work and strengthen them through gentle exercise, the tightness lets go and you feel at one with the pain, not opposed to it. The pain subsides and because you understand it, you can give your body what it needs. It's the same way when you find a hurtful habit that you want to release. There's a blues song that says, "I'm not what I want to be, but I'm better than I used to be, and I'm getting better all the time." The tendency is to put yourself down, or blame someone else for your problems. However, when you simply acknowledge this part of you, see what it wants and why it is there, then you've begun the process.

Step Two: When you accept yourself as you are right now, you become empowered to change whatever it is. There is a sense of freedom when you realize you are in the driver's seat and can let it go. However, nobody said that accepting yourself as you are is an easy thing to do and everyone struggles with this realization. Emotions can arise like shock and denial, pain and guilt, anger, and possibly depression. Lighten up. We are all perfect whatever we are and, fortunately, if you don't like your behavior you have the power to change it. Within that power of choice, you'll find sufficient energy needed to take the steps to create a happier you.

Step Three: Can you take note of where this unpleasant

behavior came from? Understand that up until now it has served a purpose. Perhaps you learned it by imitating those around you or you adopted it because you felt like you were invisible and needed to assert yourself. Was anger, stubbornness, or defensiveness a way to protect yourself or get your way when you were a kid?

When you look around at your role models was there ugly language, laziness, or bad attitudes? Did you add it to your repertoire? It's probable that you don't remember when these habits first formed, but it's likely that it happened at an early age. When you become aware that this behavior is not to your liking and you decide to change, your free will is working for your benefit. Gregg Braden writes in *The Divine Matrix*: "At every moment there are infinite possibilities of choice of how you will be or act. Making the choice is free will."[31] When you take charge, you can mold how you want to be, exhibiting your power, your potential, and respect for yourself. It might seem complicated and next to impossible, but when the change happens, it's miraculous!

Step Four: Feel good about yourself when you exercise your power. You can be someone who consciously chooses what kind of person to be and what habits to leave behind. Celebrate the person you have become.

Step Five: Know that the hard work will be worth it. Envision the negative pattern leaving your body, mind, and soul. Unfortunately, during stressful situations, the old unhealthy trait may reappear. This is the ultimate challenge. When you find yourself indulging in the behavior that you have decided to throw out, take note and stop. You will feel empowered, knowing that you were able to identify something that you wanted to change and can actually stop doing it. It is possible to break a habit, but it will probably take many attempts to eradicate this unhealthy routine. Since it has been with you for so long, it is probably a part of every cell and neural synapse in your body. Be patient. Stay vigilant, and continue to evolve. You can develop the habit of change.

Step Six: Forgive yourself when you fall back into old patterns especially in stressful situations, and have to make an adjustment again and again. For some of us, it may take a thousand run-ins with our demons to realize how deeply that habit is embedded in our psyche. Nobody is unscathed and we all need to be let off the hook. Forgiveness is a partner of unconditional love. (Let's all get out the "guilt-off spray.")

Step Seven: Seek out a mentor or a guide, someone who has gone through changes and understands what you are going through. This can be a teacher, counselor, therapist, spiritual guide, or someone who is a positive, wise, and happy role model. There's an old proverb, "When you need a teacher, s/he will be there."

Step Eight: When you acknowledge and begin work on a specific negative trait, self-respect and trust grows. Celebrate this stage of your transformation. Appreciate the hard work you've done.

> **"Love is a fabric which never fades, no matter how often it is washed in the water of adversity and grief."** Robert Fulghum

Forgive and Let Go

On the road to freedom, forgiveness unchains you from your thoughts of anger and revenge towards another person, or maybe even yourself. Letting go of past hurts does not deny or diminish the injustice, but brings peace of mind, so you are not weighed down by encumbrances and the heavy burden of holding onto grudges and even trauma. When you free yourself from harboring these negative thoughts, you begin to change your response to people, knowing they are similar to you with problems to work out. Compassion and empathy enters the picture and you can move on to live your life magnanimously.

Most parents love their children in their own way, but inevitably they botch the job. Nobody has had the perfect childhood. Everyone has experienced memorable highlights along with events that were deeply hurtful. Some of these are small hurts and, unfortunately, there are occasionally major abuses. These events in your childhood helped form your personality when they caused fear, anger, insecurity, low self-esteem, and mistrust. When you take a look at past events and see how they sculpted your childhood, you can have an insight into how these struggles gave you strength and created the amazing person you are today. On the other hand, you may find that some of your problems stem from how you reacted to those same situations. It is possible to clear out the negative aspects of your past and begin to heal that part of you that is an injured child. Becoming the parent of your inner child acknowledges and heals your child's hurts and leads to emotional health. By forgiving your parents and honoring them for doing their best, you shoulder the personal responsibility that is required to take care of yourself. Then you move forward with acceptance, forgiveness, and reconciliation.

When you become aware of the positive and negative attributes that have come down to you from your parents, you can embrace the strengths and turn the weaknesses into a source of power. *For example, like many fathers of the day, my father was a workaholic. This is a socially acceptable addiction since it put food on the table and kept a roof over the family's head. He was a surgeon and did the great work of healing people, but his busy schedule often interrupted family time. When I had children, I easily fell into the role of workaholic and super-mom. There was always so much that needed to be done, but I made a conscious decision to slow down and spend quality time with my kids while they were growing up.*

We all have our share of family problems. Parents inevitably impose hurts and their own unresolved issues onto their children. By working through and dumping this negative baggage, you can free yourself, not to mention the next generation from any painful legacy that has been passed down to you. When you do the complex work of discarding outdated, dangerous, and useless belief systems, energy is freed up to follow your passion. You can be the one to stop the mistreatment. Instead of being a victim, you will become a hero; a seeker willing to go into the deep recesses to heal the damaged person within. You may need help since these things might have been hidden and suppressed all of your life, concealed behind thick walls of fear, mistrust, and anger. Are there moats with sharks swimming around protecting you? Are they also preventing you from going into those dark, secretive places within? If your parents or caretakers were emotionally, physically, or mentally abusive, it may take professional counseling to help you find your way out of the maze of trauma that you experienced. It takes a brave and empowered person to seek the help that is needed to facilitate healing. You will not only be doing this work for yourself but for your partner, and family. If our society as a whole was more accepting and respectful of how truly difficult relationship work can be, there would not be such a stigma against asking for help.

There are healing exercises that you can do to help effect these changes. In their book, *Core Transformation*, Connirae and Tamara Andreas describe in detail the ways of delving deeply inside to heal hurts that have been hidden for years.[32] One of their exercises, for example, is to find a quiet place and become aware of yourself at each age of life from conception to the present. Become the parent to that little one, and nurture and love that child within you. Take the time to imagine yourself in the womb, cuddle and play with your one-year-old self, your two-year-old, your three-year-old, and on up to the present. Each time that you do this meditation, you might concentrate on one year of your life. Mesh with that four-year-old for instance and imagine what it was like growing up in your family. Was there tension between your parents, were you mistreated by an older sibling, and were there not enough moments of love or quality time for you in between all that was going on? There may be times when you cry for the child that is you and acknowledge your child's pain. Instead of feeling like a victim for all the hard times you experienced when you were young, you can now choose to take charge. With that decision and commitment, you become the nurturing parent to your child, treating him or her like you would have wanted to be treated, like he or she deserved.

As difficult as it may seem, you can also choose to forgive anyone who mistreated you (like your parents, teachers, or caregivers.) The freedom that you gain going through the forgiveness process will clear out the negativity residing within and set yourself up for a future of clarity and wellbeing. You don't have to forget what happened, trivialize it, or make it seem less hurtful than it was: forgiveness frees you to move forward and embrace the rest of your life. Whoever has hurt you will be metamorphosed from being the monster that haunts you, to the person who has helped you understand the true meaning of forgiveness. They have given you the impetus and strength to stand up for yourself and your new beginning.

When you feel good about having healed your wounded child, or at least are reconciled with the process, you can take the next step. This may sound strange but the next exercise is nurturing your parents at their different ages of life. Let's take it for granted that most parents suffered through many of the things that you did, if not more so. They probably believed that they were trying to do a better job of parenting than what they received. But, if they have not done any therapeutic work, they usually inflict the same mistreatment on their own kids. Unfortunately, one third of abused children grow up to be abusers.[33]

If you have developed a relationship with an empathetic partner, you can ask him/her to do these exercises with you, nurturing and loving both of you for all of your years. When you share your past with each other, it can be an incredibly empowering and healing exercise.

The intention of these exercises is not to dredge up negative, hurtful demons, but to put you in charge of caring for yourself, and bringing you to the present with a clean slate. Love fills the vacuum and you feel charged up. Things start to go your way, and magic does happen. When you wake up happy and content with your life, the interactions that you have during your day will be rewarding and synchronistic.

Two enlightening books on Forgiveness and

its effect on our health and the peace and unity of the world are from Dr. Fred Luskin, *Forgive for Good, A Proven Prescription for Health and Happiness*, and *No Future without Forgiveness* by Desmond Tutu.[34]

Catch Me Exercise

When you decide to make a change to rid yourself of a negative pattern, try something simple for starters. For instance, can you get into a habit of saying "Good Morning" to those around you, or not being rude to your family and friends? Write down exactly what change you would like to make. Then, notice when you actually do it. Did you come up with a nice response rather than your "same old, same old" routine? What did you do that was different? When these wheels are put in motion, you are working towards an attainable goal.

It's not uncommon to find yourself trying to get away with it, sort of like sneaking behind your own back? This is the "catch me" part of the exercise. Are you sabotaging yourself? Have you talked yourself into thinking that you can't do it because it is too difficult? It may be easier than you think; all you have to do is make the conscious choice. What emotions and thoughts flood through you when you try changing an old habit? We humans are instinctively bound to the status quo so you are sticking your neck out if you try. You probably need to face old hurts, acknowledge them, give them their due, forgive, and let go. That is unconditional love in action. Self-confidence increases when you treat yourself well.

> **Let reality be your guide and when you set out to live your dream, it usually becomes obvious which step to take next.**

Perspective Counts

How about the idea of (hold on to your seats) the subatomic particle theory that states, **We are all One**? All of our flesh, bones, blood, atoms, thoughts, and ideas are all one entity. We breathe the same air and drink the same water. We share the same emotions and dreams. We want the best for the earth, all sentient beings, and ourselves. Whenever you look at someone else, you are looking at yourself. If you look at another person with compassion (feeling with them), you can learn about yourself. They will become your teacher. Plutarch quoted Cato the Elder in the first century AD, **"The fool never learns from the wise man, but the wise man learns from the fool."**[35]

When life flows easily in the direction you want to go, it feels like the stars are lined up. But when life throws a major obstacle in your path, you can only resist it up to a point. You may have seen the bumper sticker: "When people make plans, God laughs." In the sailing community, we often say, "Our plans are written in the sand at low tide." Let reality be your guide and when you set out to live your dream, it usually becomes obvious which step to take next.

> **Here are five basic things that most people need for a happy life:**
> 1. You like your work.
> 2. You like who you work with.
> 3. You like who you live with.
> 4. You like where you live.
> 5. You are in good health.

Careers and Finances: Is Your Work Fulfilling?

What you choose to do for your occupation and career will, ideally, not only earn you a decent living, but it will bring you satisfaction in a job well done. In our modern world, money is the form of energy that we use to pay for our housing, school, food, clothing and incidentals. In the past, we might have bartered with the people in our village. There is even a movement afoot that uses credits to trade useful resources and skills among people in a certain area, but currently, that is the exception.

Work, sometimes referred to as one of those "four letter words," is something we all have to do to get along. Since you'll be spending a lot of your time on the job, you want to choose an occupation that is challenging, and fulfilling. Discovering your passion, acquiring the adequate training, and finding a career that captivates your interest can lead to a productive and satisfying life. It's the best when your occupation brings you pleasure, inspires you to wake up each day, and brings you a sense of joy and accomplishment. When you find the right vocation, there is enthusiasm, a sense of satisfaction, and empowerment, not to mention money in your bank account. Hard work and a passionate approach usually result in monetary wealth. Eleanor Roosevelt said, "Happiness is not a goal, it's the byproduct of right living."[36]

There is more to wage earning than merely paying the bills. It is fortuitous when your vocation fascinates you and is where your passion lies. If you are not enjoying what you do or the people you work with, and are struggling with a job that seems to be going nowhere, it will serve you well to look for better possibilities. Improving your skills to make yourself employable for a position in your chosen field may require an investment in school, including taking out loans. If you are worried about going into debt, think long and hard about your choices. Are there apprenticeships, internships, or mentoring programs where the cost is not as high? If you do decide to take out a student loan, it's like betting on yourself and who better to bet on! If you are truly following your passion, hopefully, the results will be job satisfaction and financial independence.

If you have the entrepreneurial gene, look into what it takes to start your own business, but don't quit your day job yet! In your off-hours, you can begin researching the possibilities in the fields that interest you. There are mentors who can help you traverse the thorny path of obtaining a business license, keeping track of your accounts and inventory, networking, paying taxes, hiring and maybe firing employees, applying for a business loan, and selling your product. In our town of Modesto, California, a group of mostly retired business owners use their extensive experience to help guide new entrepreneurs down the road to success.[37]

If you find yourself in an unhappy work situation or are having trouble finding a job, try making a list of your top five dream jobs. Then become proactive about pursuing what you love, while keeping your focus on your goals. Showing up every day radiating enthusiasm for work or in search of a job, even when you're doing the most mundane assignment, can make a difference. Everyone notices when you are on time, applying yourself, and are helpful to customers and co-workers. With a positive attitude, good things start happening. If your job is disagreeable, but a necessary stepping stone to a better career and a more satisfying future, can you be comfortable with it for a relatively short time, while you jump through the required hoops toward your goal?

If you haven't been able to find a job, how about volunteering for a local non-profit organization? When you are hard working and fun to be with, it is likely that a paying job will open up for you. At the very least, you will be able to network, and possibly find promising leads. When you help others, you end up helping yourself. More than likely, you will begin riding a successful wave into the future that you could only have imagined not too long ago.

You might enjoy reading Paulo Coelho's short book, *The Alchemist* about a young man who sets out to pursue his dreams. Like all of us, he needs to pay the bills and goes from one mundane job to another. With each new experience, however, he gains skills, confidence, and connections that coincidentally open doors and eventually lead to the fulfillment of life's desires.[38]

Cooperative Finances

When you bring that paycheck into a cooperative relationship, you'll find that two incomes are better than one and there might even be enough left over to fulfill your collective dreams.

Financial issues, however, can be a major cause of contention in a marriage. Statistically, money woes are the number one cause for a marriage to fall apart [affairs come in second].[39] In a survey by the Forum for Family and Consumer Issues, couples listed finances as the leading cause of marital conflict.[40]

Who brings in the pay check (s) and who pays the bills will be questions to answer as you combine your lives into one household.

Discussing your future expectations and making good agreements on how to handle your financial plans can alleviate problems. You may want to set out a one-year, five-year, and ten-year financial plan, making sure these reflect your present circumstances and your goals. Realize that when children enter the picture, (if you decide to have them), your priorities and expenses will change.

For financial information, Suze Orman's *The Nine Steps to Financial Freedom*[41] is a great book; it is concise and easy to read. She emphasizes that how you approach finances makes a difference. Worry, anxiety and reckless spending doesn't encourage abundance. Miserliness is a path to loneliness, but affluence flourishes when there is prudence and respect. When you work smarter, not harder, the results are positive.

Creating a realistic budget is a good start. The online financial spreadsheets make it easy to record all of your income in one column and expenditures in another. It becomes obvious what your expenses are when you list the rent or mortgage, and all the bills for food, clothing, gas, travel, taxes, insurance, car maintenance, and entertainment expenses. Be sure to include student loans and credit card charges. Review your budget and see if there are items you can cut to close any budget gaps. Can you consolidate and pay down your debts? It's a wise choice to pay off the debt with the highest interest rate first. Also, can you make changes in your spending habits to save up for something that you want? Decide if there will be one checking account or will you each have your own? Who will be responsible for paying the bills? How will you divide the earnings when both of you are working? Will there be a savings account? Are there retirement funds for both of you and a college fund for your children?

Usually, the home mortgage or rent will be your biggest expense. When we were buying our home in California in the 1980s, for example, the bank would not give us a mortgage if our payments would be over 30% of our income. Today, that rule has been relaxed. Over 35% of homeowners now spend more than 30% of their budget on housing. In areas of the country that have high-priced real estate, like New York or San Francisco, 20% of homeowners pay as high as 50%[42] and more. If this sounds like you, compromises may have to be made to live within your means. It can be difficult balancing the expenses with your income.

When finances are tight, be imaginative and explore ways of stretching your paycheck, coming up with a second job, or let out the entrepreneurial genie. Let creative ideas flow unimpeded, being flexible, and open-minded. Brainstorming won't cost you a dime. Can you move to a less expensive house or a less expensive area, find a higher paying job, or go back to school to upgrade your skills? Can you simplify your life in order to have time and money to pursue your dreams? It can be truly satisfying to study the numbers, make up a budget, see your debts go down, and your assets go up, and in effect, watch your dreams manifest into reality.

If you are inclined to become an entrepreneur, see a niche that needs to be filled, are you willing to "put it all in," bet on yourself, and work hard towards a goal? When you decide to start a new venture, keeping your business afloat includes following a certain format. You will be required to keep track of your income and expenditures, pay your taxes, hire employees, withhold the payroll deductions, and pay Workman's Compensation, while trying to sell your product. It will serve you well to seek out a knowledgeable CPA (Certified Public Accountant) to help you handle your taxes. Our CPA taught tax preparation at the local college so she was a savvy, well-trained ally in all of our business dealings.

*On a yearly basis, Robert and I would call an executive financial meeting of the two of us to work out our course of action for the following year. One of our arts and crafts shows where we sold our tie-dyed clothing was in Boulder City on the outskirts of Las Vegas, a nine-hour drive from home. Since there was plenty of time to talk, I would bring our accounting books along. Before we began to crunch the numbers, we let our minds wander, thinking out of the box, envisioning our future. We discussed both our short and long-range plans, like our dream to sail to Mexico aboard our sailboat, Harmony. When our children were finishing up college and becoming self-sufficient, we became serious about our dream to cruise to the tropics. We started by simplifying our lifestyle. We rarely ate out and did not renew our cable TV, magazine subscriptions, and even the local newspaper until we fulfilled our financial vision. One of the things we realized was that **it was not how much we made, but how much we spent.***

There is the old joke that you can either work forty hours a week at a job, or work eighty hours a week for yourself. *Owning our own businesses, we did have to work hard. Actual vacations were non-existent, but we made interesting stops when we traveled to the craft shows. On weekends when we didn't have fairs, we spent time in nature in nearby places like Yosemite National Park, sailing the San Francisco Bay, and exploring the California coast.*

With our large family and businesses to run, finances were often tight. I would sometimes lie awake at night mulling over how I was going to pay the bills. Robert assured me that it was okay to wake him up if I was "tripping my brains out," about the budget. Even when it was 2:00 AM, we would talk it over and come up with solutions. Then both of us could sleep peacefully. When I shared my worries, I did not feel so overwhelmed. Needless anxiety actually inhibited my thought process, stifling original and innovative ways of managing our finances. When I developed a confident attitude and believed that things would work out, energy was released and good things started to happen. Following Suze Orman's advice, I stopped worrying that I didn't have enough, and instead valued the income I had and treated it with respect and gratitude. Our finances continually improved and my sleepless nights were history.

It helped to have our kids working at the craft shows with us, and we talked openly with them about how we made, spent, and invested our income. Lively discussions were held about taxes, insurance, buying property, and the ins and outs of the world of finance. Our children knew how we paid for the groceries and the roof over their heads. In the booth, they practiced skills like dealing with the public, making change, and "closing the deal." We paid them well and they spent their earnings on clothes, transportation, and entertainment, and opened accounts for college expenses.

Rarely do two young people come into a marriage with their finances in perfect order. However, if you both have decent jobs, your economic situation will probably be comfortable. Then the ups and downs of life will come along: children, purchasing a home, job loss, illness, recessions, bad investments, etc. Ask your partner what s/he would do in these situations. Can you curtail your spending and live simply?

Are you both taking an interest in your financial affairs, even though one of you is the designated bill payer? When you share the fiscal responsibility, it helps diminish the stress and pressures that often mount over matters economical.

Do you or your partner spend compulsively? It can feel like a breach of trust when one of you buy, buy, buys, without the other's agreement. Is one partner stingy and won't allow spending for a needed vacation or a special purchase? Are there debts that need to be paid down, especially high interest credit cards? It is also good financial sense for you both to have a viable credit history so that when a big expense comes up, like buying a car or a home, both of your credit scores can be used to get a loan. When you need to decide where to invest your savings, it is helpful when you have been in the habit of talking things over and planning wisely.

If you are young, you may not be looking ahead to old age and retirement, but now's the time to start putting something (even a small amount) away in what is called a diverse portfolio of stocks, bonds, real estate, and tangibles. Then you will be covered when you want to stop working, go on some adventures, and live comfortably into that good night. With the right investments working for you, the savings will continue to accumulate when you contribute to your account on a regular basis.

Do you have a large credit card debt? The financial pundits recommend that you pay it off as quickly as possible. Ideally these cards, which generally have a high interest rate, should be used as a 30-day interest free loan and paid off entirely within the grace period. It's convenient to use your card to reserve hotel rooms and airline tickets or to purchase needed items at online stores when there are great deals. If you own your own business, you can put your everyday expenditures on the card, pay it off each month, and accumulate enough airline miles to go on a trip at the end of the year. If you are purchasing a larger item, try to pay more than the minimum payment each month. You then use the card for the convenience it offers, rather than it using you. It's a trap that can ensnare you if you are not diligent in paying this kind of debt off as quickly as possible.

Is your large debt a student loan with affordable monthly payments at a reasonable interest rate? If you are keeping up with the payments, good for you! If you happen to have a surplus, pay down the loan, especially if the interest rate is high. Can you refinance to lower your payments? Even better, look into student loan forgiveness programs that pay off the loan if you work in an under-served area.

If your biggest debt is a mortgage on a house, is it at a low interest rate? Do both of you like the home's location, size, and cost? A few years ago there was the sub-prime mortgage fiasco and many young people starting out were caught in the mess. Fortunately, there are programs to give people relief. If you wish to pay down your mortgage sooner, you can pay a little more than the minimum payment each month and you'll find yourself cutting off years of debt. Allocate the extra payment to paying down the principal of the loan.

Perhaps the debt is an indication of a larger problem, for example, compulsive spending, binge shopping, or gambling? Compulsive shopping can be an indication of deeper problems.[43] This parent/child-like struggle may prevent both of you from growing into equally responsible adults. Have a discussion about how you would budget your finances and what you would do with any discretionary income. If there is a problem, seeking financial counseling can help get your money issues on track. If one of you is careless with money it inevitably leads to financial difficulties. Balancing a checkbook, keeping track of your on line banking, and budgeting your income is rarely taught in school, but is crucial for a financially savvy relationship.

Also, when family generously lends you money for a specific purpose, such as a down payment on a home, a student loan, or a low-interest loan to help you when you are just starting out, their financial help is a sign of their support and love. Certainly, have everything put in writing. The written agreement will state the terms of the loan, the interest rate, and when and how much the monthly payments will be. Simple loan forms or promissory notes are available on the Internet.

Occasionally, loans from family members can be a mixed blessing. Is your family's financial help a way to manipulate you? Will your happiness be compromised for example, by obligations like visiting or helping out more often than is comfortable? When you talk about the details and write out any stipulations on the agreement form, you can come to an understanding that is fair for everyone.

Insurance is one of the items in your budget, right? Most states require a minimum of liability insurance for your car and collision insurance is mandatory when you are purchasing a car on credit. Likewise, a mortgage company will require proof of insurance on a home. If you are renting, purchasing renter's insurance is relatively inexpensive and can protect your possessions against theft, fire, vandalism, and water damage. In particular, life insurance is considered to be a wise investment after children are born, since the family depends on you for their support and security. Also, health insurance covers you and your family when there is sickness or hospitalization. Finally, shopping for insurance is made easier when you ask for referrals from your family or friends who have had a long history with a reputable agent.

If the two of you were raised in different economic circumstances, you will likely have different spending habits. Did you grow up in a family where money was tight, and are you worried that you will end up living in poverty again? On the other hand, did your partner come from a wealthy family or has already accumulated a fortune, accustomed to having whatever s/he desires? Are you willing to have a shared account? Are you both okay with a pre-nuptial agreement? Check with an accountant or lawyer if you have any questions.[44]

When you calculate your combined income and expenses, you can see clearly what is available for discretionary purchases. When you take worry, hassle, careless spending, and stinginess out of the equation, you'll find that your bottom line should improve. An attitude of generosity and gratitude actually works magic, returning to you in abundance.

Making agreements about the big financial expenditures, like buying a car or home, will challenge your ability to talk things through and come to a satisfying compromise. When you discuss possibilities, share your dreams, and evaluate the pros and cons, you usually make the right choices. Let's take purchasing a home as an example. The "smart money" doesn't buy real estate in an inflated market where homes are going for more than the asking price. Wait for the inevitable swing in prices and buy when properties become more affordable. If you are handy, you can buy a fixer-upper at a reasonable price, and then put your sweat equity into making this shipwreck into a dreamboat.

Here are a few guidelines to determine how much of a mortgage you will be able to carry at this time. According to Moneying.com, it is financially viable to buy a house if you plan on living in it for at least five years and the PITI (mortgage principal, interest, taxes and insurance) is affordable.[45] Is this a favorable time in the housing market to buy? Is there enough saved up for a down payment, with wages coming in monthly to cover the mortgage payment and pay your other bills? Is this where you want to settle down? Will your job require your family to relocate any time soon?

If you move to a new town, it is a good idea to rent for a year before you decide to buy. Renting a home allows you time to accumulate enough savings for a down payment while making sure that this area is where you want to live. If you have children, are good schools close by? Is there easy access to work and shopping, and a warm community feeling with welcoming neighbors? Do you have family living in the area?

When you come up to the big decisions, are both of you on the same page? It may feel stressful, but by working together you can be satisfied with your choices. Is one of you tight with money? Are you scared to commit to the payments and the upkeep of a home? When you talk about major expenditures, it helps if you are both organized with your finances and flexible when you do your brainstorming. An excessively cautious partner can stifle an adventurous move, while risk takers can make mistakes and cause havoc to the family's security. Success usually follows if a visionary entrepreneur is allowed to pursue his dreams while his partner keeps a close eye on the spending. It helps to discuss your plans with trustworthy family and/or friends who are knowledgeable about things financial.

A few tips can change your purchasing habits and set you up for prosperity. For instance, try to negotiate the most reasonable terms if you have to buy on credit. If you save up beforehand and pay in full when you make the purchase, you can often bargain for a better deal with cash in hand. It's good to remember: It's not how much you make, but how much you spend. Can you stay within the budget?

Finally, there are books, seminars, and workshops about finances that are available. Can someone from your family or circle of trusted friends recommend a good financial advisor? Suze Ormond,[46] who has already been mentioned, has written several books and Dave Ramsey's[47] *The Total Money Makeover* is also an easy read with a no-nonsense, balanced attitude about financial matters. These books have helped us manage our resources, and we appreciate their excellent advice.

The Power Struggle

Financial issues are a leading cause of upsets, and then there are times, when something weird triggers arguments that erupt out of the ether. These hassles can leave you feeling weakened and vulnerable, with your potency and competence leaking away. At this point compromise is the name of the game and you begin to search for that place that brings satisfaction to both of you. What you are trying to do is include each other in the decision-making process, which then creates the synergy that empowers you both.

Power struggles can show up in loud, knockdown, drag-out confrontations or as quiet manipulations where one partner works behind the scenes to have it his/her way. When the energy is leeched from the relationship, you feel mistreated. The intensity of the energy is the same as your happiest moments, but is now in opposition rather than cooperation.

How you interact in the car for example, can be a comical or maybe not so funny indication of what is going on. The question is "Who is steering?" Are you the conscientious driver or the helpful navigator? Can you exchange positions easily? Occasionally, the stress of driving can bring out the worst in you. Are you being stubborn and disrespectful, driving too fast with a touch of road rage, making moves that scare your passenger? Gaining power through fear will not serve you well. Or, is the back seat driver distrustful, having a hard time relaxing even though you have things under control? Is s/he constantly giving directions like, "Stop at the light," "Look Out!" "Turn here," "Take that exit," when you are perfectly capable of making your way through town? All of this inevitably makes for an uncomfortable trip. If this sparring is going on in your car, you can be sure that it is also happening elsewhere in your relationship.

Power struggles mostly center around control dramas. James Redfield in *The Celestine Prophecy*[48] describes how in the middle of an argument, we tend to revert back to childhood ways of getting what we want. Inevitably this builds animosity and distance between two people who are supposed to be in love. Control issues occur when someone has to have it a certain way. They also don't want to end up feeling insignificant, unempowered, and invisible. The four control dramas that are described by Redfield are Intimidation, Interrogation, Aloofness, and Poor-Me. When someone is being intimidating, for example, it might spark the poor-me routine, locking in the drama. If you are aloof, your partner might get into the interrogation mode to try to find out what you're thinking. To jump on the opposite end only intensifies the problem and leaves you both unsatisfied. The wedge becomes wider and the struggle continues.

There is a way to side step these soap operas. Even though it takes two to tango, the only thing you truly have control over is yourself. You can dance the night away, or you can step all over each other's feet. You might stop for a minute and practice a step or two, or you can sadly choose not to dance at all. In this particular case, you can identify the control drama and say, "I am feeling intimidated by you. Is that how you want me to feel?" or "You are feeling aloof. Do you want me to leave you alone?" Stating it clearly defines and untangles the loop. Subconsciously, your partner probably doesn't have a clue that he is acting this way, or that his behavior is negatively affecting you. When you say what it is and how it feels to you, then you can begin to stop the power struggle.

It is possible to reach a balance where the power and decision making is shared. You might want to revisit the chapters on **Communication** and **The Subconscious**.

When the energy is lined up, and you aren't trying to control each other, you can recapture the vibrant, joyful, optimistic spark. It might take several sessions, but it can be done. Just try not to do it while you're driving; it's dangerous enough out there. It is possible to return to that peaceful place smarter and happier, and with less emotionally upsetting theatrics.

Drawing the Line

Some days you feel like you're so in love with the perfect partner, and the next thing you know, you're embroiled in a hassle that seemed to come out of nowhere. Let's say that you've been together for a while and things have become ho-hum, mundane, or distant. Although you've tried to keep current and work things out, changes haven't been forthcoming and the stresses have worn a tear in the fabric of your relationship. Issues have surfaced that remain unresolved. Does your guy continue to flare up in anger? Has your gal become snarky and stubborn, refusing to change her attitude? Has he been drinking too much again, or is it (yikes) obvious that she has been having an affair? Enough is enough, and you decide to so something (anything) to make it better. It's time to up the ante. You might first consider a consultation with a recommended marriage counselor. It would be best if both of you could attend, but how about scheduling a session for yourself and see where that takes you? This is where you clearly define what you can't live with anymore and how you want your future to be. Hopefully, it's an easier fix than you think, but folks often resist this kind of help. What are you going to do?

When you decide that the situation has become too dangerous and toxic for you and your family, you stand up for yourself; you "Draw the Line," and insist that life be good. You want your partner to know that his/her behavior is too destructive to live with and you have decided to separate for now. If there is no concerted effort to alter the downhill course, there will be consequences! Now, can you agree to go to counseling?

For sure, you are initiating a high-risk maneuver. You don't want to lose him or her, and destroy everything that you have worked so hard to create. It's common to think you have failed, and that it's going to feel even worse when everyone finds out about it. But you are doing this for your own sanity, and if you have children, for them. Even though you are frightened by the prospect of what you are about to do, you need to act decisively. Tough love is standing up to your partner so that eventually your relationship can thrive. You are the only one who can give this ultimatum, and unfortunately you can't predict whether it will make or break your partnership. If nothing changes and you've asked him to leave and he refuses, then you are the one who has to find another place to stay. It might even be your house, but right now we are talking about something that is much bigger than material possessions. The "stuff" will all be sorted out eventually.

Making a decisive move elevates you into a powerful position. You can feel courage rushing through your veins, and fear and insecurity fade into the background. Self-esteem rises when you take control of your life, giving you strength to handle any storm. With your newly found confidence, you can turn an unhappy situation into personal growth. Your friends and family have seen you suffer and will want to support you. They see the situation from a less emotional viewpoint than you do, and they want you to be happy.

After you've put your foot down, there are several possible outcomes. S/he could walk out of the house and never come back. Or, your partner begs you to give him or her another chance, but unfortunately continues to hold on tightly to the same destructive habits with no real commitment to make amends. And then, thankfully, there is the partner who comes back and wants to listen respectfully and do whatever is necessary to make it work and backs up his claims with action.

There are attitudes that you can adopt while waiting for things to develop that will keep your unconditional love flowing. It helps if you can have a frame of mind that is not attached to your partner coming back. It's not the time to be clingy, desperate, or act like a victim. Keeping the attitude "I love you and want you to be with me," while remaining tough, holding out for a sincere change, may be one of the hardest things you've ever done. Though you cannot live with your partner because of how you are being treated, assure him that your love is still solid. It is undoubtedly difficult for him to make this big adjustment. When he decides to make a commitment to get it together, assure him that you are patiently waiting, your door remains open, and your welcoming love will be there. However, if he insists on staying in the old patterns, that door will eventually close and you will move on. You have no power to change anyone but yourself. It is his decision, his choice alone.

  At this juncture, there can be a period of living apart. A separation can certainly lead to divorce, but more importantly taking a temporary break might help turn your relationship around. During this time, there is a rediscovery of your individual selves and you see life from a different perspective. A realization comes that this drama wasn't entirely your partner's doing, and you might even begin to see where you contributed to at least half of the problem. After taking some time apart, for a few days, a week, a month, or even six months, it usually becomes obvious if the relationship can be revived. Whether your partner returns with a sincere commitment to change his unacceptable behavior or you end up losing a toxic partner, either way you have now rocked the boat, taken a stand, and you will feel empowered to be at the threshold of a more positive phase of life.

  If your partner has had that epiphany that he loves you, and doesn't want to lose you, and is willing to make the necessary changes and do whatever it is that you are requesting, this is the magic moment you've been waiting for. Things feel good again and the possibilities are endless, but there are agreements to solidify for the relationship to continue. Talking with a marriage counselor or trusted third party is usually one of the requirements before he moves back in. Does your partner need to go to anger management classes or rehab for an addiction? Rewiring the relationship so that it is good for you will take time. Allow the reconciliation to unfold. It should feel truly wonderful.

When you allow your partner to move back in, he will not be perfect. Who is? Be receptive when he makes amends, because this is his chance to prove to you that he is working on changing the old patterns. A slice of humble pie mixed with an earnestness to delve into problem areas, making sincere apologies, with a willingness to listen to feedback is on the menu of the day.

When your partner goes through a transformation, there's a good chance that the next change that is needed will then be your own. If a chair is wobbly and you trim one of the legs, inevitably, another leg becomes unsteady and needs shaving as well. You have your issues too! When the loud, obvious difficulties are taken care of, subtler problems emerge. The artichoke has many layers. After the leaves with appetizer bites of goodness, comes the fuzzy, pokey stuff to spoon out, leaving a delicious "heart" in the middle. Changing for each other will continue to be the building blocks of your relationship - a lifelong process to continually create the love you deserve.

You Did What? You had an Affair?

Uh, Oh! What a fine mess you have gotten into. It's become complicated and, of course, the sex was wonderful. If you are feeling dissatisfied with your relationship, talk it out before you jump into another person's arms! Are there children who will be affected? What you are doing is devastating to these innocent ones. Have you gone the extra mile like going to counseling to try to work things out to a satisfying makeover of your relationship? Through this process, you may find that your marriage is over, and has been for a while. In which case, you can leave honorably and move on with your life. If you can wait to have an affair until after things have come to an agreed upon finale, it shows respect for your partner, yourself, and your relationship. It lessens the feelings of jealousy and betrayal, and can somewhat alleviate the intensity of the already difficult process of divorce. Unfortunately, being the promiscuous Homo sapiens that we are, many of us do not think that far ahead before we act.

Your marriage was going along beautifully at first, but things have changed. The sheen has worn off and your life together has become routine. Has a child been born which takes up the time that you used to spend with your sweetheart? Are you feeling frustrated because things are not how they should be? Are there money problems? Is your career stagnant? Has romance flown out the window and your love life lost its sparkle? Is there someone at work who is flirting with you and you are enjoying a break from the same old, same old? Dissatisfied as you are, what the heck, and you sneak it in.

Afterwards, with your mind racing and the smell of your lover swirling in the air, you realize how compromised it feels. Yes, you enjoyed yourself, but complications are setting in. Your partner acts cool to you; s/he knows (they always know) that something happened, and questions you about where you have been. It makes you nervous to live a lie and there are conflicted feelings about what to do next. While the person you are having an affair feels like your new soul mate, you do not feel like destroying your family. It was not supposed to be like this! If only you could have your cake and eat it too, but that is just not happening. A serious breach of trust has occurred. Where do you go from here?

Eventually, your partner finds out. You have no control over how your partner will take the news and what will happen next. Perhaps your not-so-friendly mate might be grateful for the truth. Unfortunately, s/he will also be extremely hurt and angry. What you both do next will decide whether your marriage continues or not. Will s/he not be able to accept you having an affair and demand a divorce?

If a couple understands that the transgression is an indication that there has been a breakdown in the marriage, you have the option to call it quits or rededicate yourself to the hard work of repairing it from the foundation up. In addition to the hurt of betrayal and the breach of trust, there are the underlying problems that made having an affair imaginable in the first place. These issues have stacked up over the years. The warm loving spark that was there when you were first together has become an inflammatory, dangerous, negative conflagration. If you can somehow switch back to the original positive love that you once had, there is a chance to make it work. A professional counselor or therapist can, of course, help you sort out what exactly the issues are. One way or another, you will each have to understand, acknowledge, and accept your role in the situation before deciding how to proceed.

Is it time for a separation? Time away from each other gives each of you a chance to think about who you are as individuals and what each of you truly wants. If you decide you want to preserve your marriage, there are issues to be worked out now and on a regular basis. Does your partner say s/he is sorry so many times that you finally forgive him/her? When both of you are serious about working through the destruction and hurt, your marriage will have traversed the dark night of the soul and come out into a rejuvenated morning. It takes love, trust, respect, compassion, tenderness, and dedication to fix a broken heart.

While you are still separated, would an old fashioned date be possible? Do you look forward to being with each other again? Can you go to a movie or have a nice dinner and rekindle the passion that you once had? Can it feel like old times, enjoying that turned on feeling again? Can you reach a satisfactory resolution about the issues that caused the problem in the first place? In that case, you sound like you are on the road to a new beginning. Best of luck to you both, and keep the love flowing through the ups and downs.

In a stable and compassionate partnership, working it out and changing for each other becomes part of the routine. Issues are brought up and processed with respect. It doesn't mean that things don't sometimes get heated, but when the agreement is to work it through until you reach satisfaction, trust is built up again and the ugly feelings disappear.

The other possibility is you've decided to separate or file for a divorce. One shattered person is left behind, while the other shattered person walks out the door. He or she feels hurt, angry, bewildered, jealous, betrayed, shamed, neglected, and abandoned. Self-esteem has been relegated to the basement and feelings of worthlessness blur the vision.

Life does march on, however, and there is a grieving process to go through that enables you to move forward. In a quiet spot far away from anyone, cry, scream, or pound on a pillow! Go deep into the very depths of your being. The trees, the sky, the birds and the flowers are your companions. Then, instead of wallowing in your victimhood, take care of your immediate needs and once again begin to live life to the fullest. No one wants to be with someone who is too despondent to feel joy or is occasionally spewing venom. With the help from your support team of family, friends, and preferably, a counselor, begin the difficult job of letting go of the past, learning from your mistakes, and rebuilding your confidence.

Until you take time to study the lessons of your recent heartache, you are bound to repeat the pattern. Resist the tendency to run into someone else's arms in a rebound romance. After all, you allowed the issues in your relationship to build up to this drama. Consider this fiasco a positive step, launching you into a more fulfilling life. If the separation is amicable, you and your family can heal and move beyond the pain. There can be acceptance and forgiveness. No doubt you also have a lot of work to do, like settling finances and that child custody discussion.

It is sad when divorces are ugly, especially when they involve children. Christine Northrup, in her book *The Wisdom of Menopause*,[49] writes about how she made the best of her situation. She and her ex-husband agreed to meet for lunch after the divorce was finalized and she thanked him for their two wonderful children, and all the good times they had together. When a couple can arrive at a peaceful place, their children have an easier time adjusting.

Breaking Up is Hard to Do

The romance was intense and incredibly gratifying, but then somehow things started to deteriorate, implode, and finally fall apart. What happened to that turned-on love that was so wonderful in the beginning? Where is that person who you wanted to be with every minute of the day and for the rest of your life? Did the flowers wilt and the kisses become non-existent? (There's still passion but it's gone to the dark side). Usually, the first impulse is to say that it is your partner's fault. She changed for the worse, or I changed and she stayed the same, or we went our separate ways. Was one of you not ready for a serious relationship? In that case, did the other push too hard for it to happen? Was someone just out for a good time with no intention of really living up to a commitment? If you end up dumped and disempowered, with your energy depleted, can you take some responsibility for having chosen this scenario that spiraled down into emptiness and animosity? What can you do? Once the crying and anguish subsides, and you have pulled yourself together, you might chalk it up to Life Experience 101. As Deepak Chopra wrote in *Creating Affluence*, "in reality, there is no such thing as failure. What we call failure is just a mechanism through which we can learn to do things right.[50]

Fortunately, there are things you can do. Can you leave this toxic relationship behind and learn from your mistakes? When you decide to separate, can you leave on good terms and not allow your anger and resentment to fester? You don't want to build up insurmountable walls that will prevent you from being civil in the future. These choices require contemplation and forgiveness. You can let go and move on, gaining understanding and resiliency from life's curve ball.

Couples inevitably come to this crossroad. Is your relationship worth it or is it time to break up? If there is a major flaw like domestic violence, addiction, or infidelity, with no remorse or effort to repair the problem, it may be time to admit that it is OVER.

There are a few precautions as you move on. Take it slow. Before you jump into a relationship again, take stock of what you have just been through and learn from your mistakes. In the meantime, live life to the fullest. When you can empty your heart of resentment, guilt, anger, and pain, you'll have a resilient and sturdier foundation, which will take you into deeper friendships.

Fortunately, time is on your side. Often, there is a tendency to rebound, feeling that you need to fill that huge hole that has been left in the wake of breaking up. Give yourself plenty of space to contemplate the changes that you have gone through. What could you have done differently? Why did you choose that person in the first place and ignore the red flags? If you forgo this process, answering these questions and figuring out the whys, etc., you're likely to jump back into a similar situation. Learn about who you are and clear out some of the blockages that keep you from finding the love that you truly want and deserve.

If two people decide to permanently separate, healing can happen after all is said and done. You might be able to meet on neutral ground and celebrate the time that you spent together. Let him/her know how grateful you are for the good times, the positive lessons, the adventures, and the love you experienced. If you can let the relationship go in peace, you will both be happier people for it. When there are children involved, your future meetings for scheduled weekends, graduations, weddings or birthdays will be cordial and the children will suffer less. It is already hard enough on the kids; let's not make it worse.

Joint Custody and a Single-Parent Home

Sometimes our lives don't evolve like we imagined. Things happen and there can be separation and divorce. Children are affected by these major storms of life, and it's imperative that we do the best we can to give them the opportunities to succeed. Because of our high divorce rate in the United States, 35% of our kids are being brought up in single parent families.[51]

It's more common than ever that children are raised in a joint custody situation in which both Mom and Dad are involved in their development. Having two parents in a child's life is usually a positive influence. Just because two adults can't live together doesn't mean that they aren't still responsible and caring partners in raising their offspring.

Unfortunately, a disproportionate number of these kids suffer from neglect and experience difficulty in school. A high dropout rate can lead to low paying jobs and the downward spiral of poverty.[52] To reverse this trend, it would serve us well to be prepared to face the challenge of keeping marriages together. Even after kids enter the picture, counseling and classes on relationships and the art of raising children would be invaluable. There are wonderful guidebooks, many of which are in the bibliography of this book. The family is best served when our children are given a chance for a promising and happy future.

A divorced or separated single parent, often the mother, should receive adequate child support from her former partner. Unfortunately, many single mothers with children have to resort to legal means to receive what is due when it is not forthcoming. The best-case scenario is when things are worked out respectfully, without involving lawyers and nasty, expensive legal battles. When the issues are settled, put all of your energy into making life good for you and your family.

If your child is living with Mom and does not have the influence of his father, positive male influences in his life are needed to round out his early experiences. A trusted grandfather, uncle or friend might take him under his wing and teach him values and skills from their male perspective. If your child is mostly living with his father, there could be a grandma, aunt, or friend to relate to him/her from the female point of view. Sometimes male teachers at elementary, middle and high school grade levels can be positive male role models. Your child will appreciate it when you put in a request for a certain teacher who is going to be a good fit. You may not always receive your first choice, but more often than not, the administration accommodates parents concerned about the welfare of their child. Hopefully, parents also have a warm community of family, friends, and neighbors who can be relied on to be a village. If all of our children can be given opportunities and positive paths to choose from, everyone benefits. Check out *The Co-Parenting Tool Kit: The Essential Supplement for Mom's House, Dad's House for Kids* by Isolina Ricci, Ph.D.[53]

Keeping the Romance Hot

Whew! You've made it through a few rough times but you're still together and your intimacy has a depth that wasn't there before your latest challenges.

With the garbage sorted out and your heads clear, happiness blossoms. Appreciation, gratitude, and celebration keep your romance sparkly day-by-day and year-to-year. When simple things like a thank you for doing a round of dishes, taking out the garbage, or cooking a meal are a part of your daily routine, your thoughtfulness provides the positive energy and affirmation that keeps you both energized and on top of the world. Everyone likes to be complimented for what they do. When you can spontaneously drop everything for a hug or a walk to the park, you reconnect and your day is invigorated. Random acts of kindness keep a marriage dynamic. Spontaneous things like a shoulder rub or a rose picked from the yard set your day on a high plane.

Each person from an early age has a language of love that fills his/her needs. In Gary Chapman's *Five Languages of Love, The Secret to Love that Lasts,* he describes how when we are loved in the way that truly satisfies our soul, our emotional tank is replenished and we have an easier time handling life's stresses.[54]

The five languages are:
1. Affirmation
2. Quality Time
3. Touch
4. Service
5. Gifts

Our family enjoyed playing a game with these five love language options. There were about 10 of us ranging from grandparents, parents, grandchildren, and adults without children. We each had a paper and pen and rated the five languages in order of importance to us. Then we went around the circle and everyone tried to guess what the top two languages were for each person. We all kept track of our guesses. The grandkids were as engaged as anyone and liked to see if their language was chosen accurately. Although some people intuitively guessed correctly, others weren't as accurate, and there were a few surprises.

When a child is acting up for instance, if his #1 language is touch, a light massage can calm the situation. Giving affirmation to a husband can make him feel loved, appreciated, and respected. If someone is not a touchy, feely person, for instance, he may appreciate taking a long walk, or maybe receiving a romantic gift. Or, can you do one of those five-minute jobs on the to-do list that brightens your partner's day?

Little kids love to laugh and dance around in uninhibited splendor. They are excited about what parents perceive as the most inconsequential things. Unfortunately, our youthful exuberance is ground down by life's struggles, but the enthusiasm can be somewhat recaptured with gratitude and appreciation. When your sweetheart fixes something like the leak under the sink and you take a moment from your busy schedule to celebrate the triumph, you pump up the connection. He may not always show his love with hugs and showers of kisses, but he does put his all into stopping that drip. His ingenuity, skill, and those seven trips to Home Depot are demonstrating his devotion. When you thank him for his effort, he is turned on by your sweet attention.

Most women adore flowers, hugs, and compliments, and a reticent guy may need to step out of an old comfort zone to let her know how wonderful she is. Everyone wants to be respected and appreciated for the things that they do. When you take the time, even briefly, to acknowledge each other's efforts, gratitude abounds.

Part 2. The Art of Raising Children

Back in the summer of 1971, our old school bus was parked with the rest of the Caravan under the tall oak, poplar, and hickory trees on a friend's 650 acres of undeveloped land south of Nashville. In that pastoral setting, The Farm midwives delivered our first child. In the next twelve years, this competent team of midwives was soon to become well known and respected internationally. They helped me deliver our children in my own bed. Each birthing was an amazingly empowering and life affirming experience, the best possible way we could have imagined to have our babies enter the world, surrounded by love, support and soft lighting.

When children enter your world, no one can adequately explain how your lives will be changed. Busy, yes, sleepless nights, yes, less time for yourself, yes, and also selflessness, dedication, patience, consistency, resiliency, flexibility, youthful exuberance, playfulness, and a sense of humor become some of the characteristics that fit your new parental job description. It helps to have common agreements about values and discipline in order to manage the family as a cohesive and united team. With less tension the children prosper. Different styles of parenting show the kids that life can be handled in various ways. This is fine as long as there is a consistent mutual understanding about boundaries and consequences.

Parents want to do their best to raise their children to be healthy and happy, capable of taking care of themselves when they grow up and strike out on their own. However, the subconscious tendency is to raise your children the same way that your parents raised you. How did your parents treat you, both positively and negatively? While celebrating the positive gifts, changing any negative patterns might require delving into unhappy memories. In the book, *Core Transformation* by Connirae and Tamara Andreas,[55] there are exercises to help you take over the parenting of your inner child. When you give the hurt or misunderstood child that lives within you the love, tenderness, and nurturing that was absent when you were young, you can transfer that same compassionate care to your own kids. It feels good when you treat them like you always wished you had been treated. Making agreements with your partner to work on changing harmful patterns of parenting goes a long way to reinforce a positive family life. When you change negative behavior, you remove a legacy that would otherwise be passed on to the next generation. Knowing how you want to raise your children will make it easier when issues arise. Creating positive patterns in your family will give your children and your descendants the most valuable gift you can possibly imagine.

Young kids are eager to explore their world to its limits and try out all sorts of things that test their boundaries. Be cautious when giving a young child too much leeway, allowing him to run his own show. Children don't yet have the knowledge and understanding to know what is safe and best for them, and inevitably will feel overwhelmed with the burden of responsibility beyond their maturity. When reasonable limits are made clear and enforced with consistency, there is more time to engage in constructive and fun activities.

Youngsters quickly become our mirrors. If there is a problem with your little one, you can often find a similar behavior within yourself. If you can moderate your actions, you'll find the behavior will often fade away in your kids. Living consciously and being willing to modify any egregious conduct will provide children with a favorable environment to grow up in where they can explore, make mistakes, and evolve. Also, when parents celebrate their love for each other, children learn about caring. When parents can apologize (after all even Mom and Dad blow it sometimes), children grow up with empathy for others. When your toddler for instance, tests his boundaries (it is what kids do), being consistent and setting appropriate limits may require great effort, but your child will feel safe and secure.

Children love to hear the truth. Any time you give your kids an accurate view of life, it helps them understand our complex world, which will pay off handsomely in the future. They eagerly soak up information when it is at their level of understanding. Encouraging a child's natural curiosity and zest for discovery is mutually rewarding. Travel, for example, is a wonderful way to show children the world and stimulate their imaginations. Visiting museums, concerts, libraries, and trips out into nature inspires and energizes the whole family.

When your children know that you will help them find the answers to their most challenging questions, they come to you in search of knowledge. If there is a lot of "Don't bother me, I'm busy," or "because I said so," you push your children away to seek out their answers elsewhere. It wasn't always easy, but in our family, we talked openly about finances, world events, taxes, politics, religion, death, birth, sex, drugs, and any other subject that our children asked about.

On a long drive home from a craft fair, our son started asking us about our rental properties and how to buy a house. The discussion turned to mortgages, title companies, capital gains, loans, and PITI (Principal, Interest, Taxes, Insurance) that make up a monthly payment. Helping him learn this new language may have paved a way for his future real estate investments. We tried to be consistently honest, and our children trusted us to tell them the truth. If we didn't know the answer, we would look it up in our second-hand set of Encyclopedia Britannica or make a trip to the library. In this age of instant information, when our grandchildren have a question, we don't hesitate to "ask the phone."

Parents also have a choice of what spiritual orientation you want for your children and the values that you consider important. How will you approach those mysterious questions that children love to ask like, "Where do I come from?" or "Where do I go when I die?" Are you and your partner in agreement on these subjects or can you give your children two different ways to look at life? It helps if both of you can express your inner perspectives and give your children a solid foundation to stand on, while they develop their own beliefs and values.

If you were raised in a happy, loving family, then you have respected role models to follow when it comes to rearing your own children. However, if you were brought up in a somewhat dysfunctional family, you may have to search out mentors, counselors, or parenting classes that can show you ways to create a warm, well-functioning household. There are numerous books written by experts to help guide you along the path of raising a child, but the key ingredient is a mother and father who love and respect each other. If you are a single parent, having love and respect for yourself will bring success. The medium is the message. It is not what you say, but what you do.

Mahatma Gandhi, a "Householder Yogi"

How can parents create a home that enriches each member of the family, where love is the active ingredient and happiness is the norm? One of Mahatma Gandhi's revolutionary ideas was the concept of the "Householder Yogi." His premise was that rather than reaching enlightenment by sitting in an ashram, the householder yogi supports the family, nurtures the relationship with his or her spouse, has integrity in business, and helps raise the children.

One of Gandhi's well known quotes was, "If we are to teach real peace in this world,...we shall have to begin with the children."[56]

Basically, everything that you do is the *yoga*. Each person finds their own path and decides how their meditation and practice will be.

Below are more relevant quotes from Gandhi:

"Be the change you want to see in the world."

"Live as if you were to die tomorrow, Learn as if you were to live forever."

"Happiness is when what you think, what you say, and what you do are in harmony."

"The weak can never forgive. Forgiveness is the attribute of the strong."

"Continue to grow and evolve."

"Take care of the moment, change yourself, you are in control."

"In a gentle way, you can shake the world."

"Dreams at first seem impossible, then seem improbable, and finally, when we commit ourselves become inevitable."

"The future depends on what we do in the present."

"Your beliefs become your thoughts,
 Your thoughts become your words,
 Your words become your actions,
 Your actions become your habits,
 Your habits become your values,
 Your values become your destiny."[57]

The Birthing -- Welcome to the Planet

When we were part of the spiritual community, we had an agreement to live a healthy lifestyle by staying away from tobacco, alcohol, and non-organic drugs like meth, opioids and cocaine, which also incidentally included birth control pills. I discontinued the pill and had three boys in four years and then three girls not long afterwards. People used to joke, "Don't you own a TV?" Several years later, we did have an old black and white TV run on a trickle charge battery, but who had time to watch it? I could have had an abortion, and several of my relatives encouraged it; however, it was the last thing on my mind. Life is precious, and I felt it within me at each conception. Once I started having children, I gave them my all. Raising them was the most rewarding, happy, love-filled, difficult, painful, satisfying, and challenging experience I've ever had. The ultimate extreme sport is raising children.

The time of conception was a beautiful, joyous moment. The love that existed between Robert and I was real, tangible, and magical, and was passed on to this emerging human being. I never doubted that a soul was within me, and I loved it before I could feel the first kick. Later, when I would lie down to rest, the baby would know that I was focused on him and he would become active, responding to my touch. When Robert put his hand on my belly he could feel the baby moving around.

When I was pregnant, it felt like I was an embodiment of Mother Earth: at one with nature, grounded in love, and a carrier of new life. Lovemaking was great during pregnancy; my breasts were full and sensitive to the touch. It was easy to get turned on, and it was okay for us to gently make love. An extra benefit was there were no worries that I would become pregnant!

I had pre-natal check-ups at The Farm Clinic once a month, and weekly during the final month. The midwives not only checked out how the baby was developing, but how I was feeling and how my husband and I were getting along. They knew that the birthing would be easier if problems were worked out and, as a couple, we were in sync.

When you become pregnant, figuring out where and how to have your baby becomes your primary focus. Everyone looks forward to having a positive experience. Ina May Gaskin's *Spiritual Midwifery* and her *Guide to Childbirth*[58] are two valuable, instructional books for present day mothers and midwives. Also, her recently released movie, *Birth Story: Ina May Gaskin and The Farm Midwives*[59] is insightful and inspiring. She gives helpful advice to Mom and Dad, about all the options available. Whether you have your baby at home, a birthing center, or at a hospital, after reading Ina May's books, you can go into the birthing well prepared and knowing what to expect. Another movie that was an eye-opener about modern day birthings was Ricky Lake's *The Business of Being Born.*[60] Two of our daughter-in-laws made the decision to have home births after seeing this movie.

Including your partner in the amazing experience of pregnancy is what he needs. Share your feelings. The baby is the fruit of your relationship and the closer the two of you become, the easier the birthing and the raising of your child will be.

When a baby comes into an environment where everyone treats the birthing as a sacred passage, she is imprinted with respect and awe. The vibrations are shimmering and the air is electric. Giving birth becomes an awesome life-changing experience.

Move over world, a new soul, a holy child, a perfect Buddha has arrived. Each birthing is a mystical and spiritual experience that welcomes a baby onto Planet Earth. A newborn brings intuitive knowledge and survival instincts, like knowing how to suck, and grab your finger with her little hands. When you spend mellow time with your new baby you sense her high level of intelligence, telepathy, and awareness. She brings with her a pure Zen beginner's mind, and becomes an extraordinary teacher. She responds with gurgles, smiles, kicks, and long moments of eye contact. Your newborn soon begins to understand her world through her senses and experiences, and by what you teach her.

Baby needs to be physically and emotionally close to her parents. Not long ago, she was in the womb, warm, secure, nurtured, and protected. When she comes into the world, your touch is her warmth and security. Mama also welcomes the bonding as much as baby does, and hugging and cuddling usually comes naturally. Breastfeeding enhances the connection, easing the pain of the still contracting uterus as it returns to its normal size. Besides the sustenance, vitamins, and immunity your baby receives from breast milk, she also is nurtured with emotional and physical contact from her mother. If breast-feeding is not an option, you can still share the close physical contact when you bottle-feed your infant. To ensure this close connection, can you take enough time off from work to be with this precious newborn?

The extended family also shows its strength, helping the new mother after the birth. You can actually find time to relax for a minute, knowing that your baby is in the care of people you trust. While grandparents cook, do the laundry and dishes, you can spend time with your little one. When Mom needs a break, a shower, or a nap, grandma and grandpa will be more than happy to spend time with the newest edition to their family.

I had my babies on The Farm at home in our own bed. By the time my labor began to heat up, there was a doctor on call, and an ambulance parked outside of our front door in case of an emergency. Robert literally and figuratively was behind me, helping to neutralize the intensity of my contractions. When our last child Olivia was born, for example, he was my strength, with his firm touch, soft kisses, gentle persuasion, and encouraging words. He was one with me as I contracted and pushed the baby out into the world. The midwives immediately placed Olivia on my breasts and she began sucking while they tended to the umbilical cord and the delivery of the placenta. My new baby was still a part of me while she was having her first glimpse of the world. Our bonding was immediate and complete. Later that night, Robert wrapped her warmly in a blanket, and carried her outside in the October chill and showed her the night sky with the full moon shining brightly.

When my first daughter, Audrey, cried, she let me know that she was awake and hungry. When I would go over to her, I'd whisper, "I am here now, you can stop crying." And most of the time she settled down. I would then change her diaper and nurse her. I felt that she sensed what I was saying; the telepathic connection that was possible with my babies always amazed me.

I was with my newborns for the first six months, before returning to part-time work. While I was home, I watched children for other working mothers and, fortunately, I was able to take my nursing baby with me to my job. Having a family and community to support you during this time, to bring you meals, give you breaks, and let you know how to navigate this new stage in life is truly a wonderful gift.

The Newborn

Your new baby is tougher than you think. That's already been proven when she survived the intense birth process. Every newborn makes an impact, and the earth shifts over to accommodate her. Changes happen around the high energy of a baby's arrival. Your little one is so pure, bringing a fresh outlook on life. An extended family is usually eagerly awaiting this grand event and ready to support Mom and Dad.

A small infant's physical growth rate is remarkable, and each day her mental ability and senses develop. She grows so quickly, doubling her weight in six months and tripling it within a year. Soon she is responding with a smile, her eyes sparkling with deep knowledge and understanding. Even the air around you and your newborn can become energized with waves of shimmering light, like the famous artists' renditions of the mother and child.

Sometimes, too many well-meaning visitors can fatigue mother and baby who are in a high state of consciousness and vulnerability. Perhaps a close family member can act as the gate, fielding phone calls, answering the door, and making sure that the parents can rest up after the birthing. The sisterhood of mothers, aunts, sisters, and friends might share in the chores, allowing Dad more time to be a part of his expanded family. The brotherhood can also participate by helping the new father with errands and provide emotional support and camaraderie. It makes sense to have cooperative family connections when the new member of your family arrives. If you have this kind of assistance, consider yourself lucky.

After the birthing, your Mama hormones are changing over from supporting a life within you to producing nourishing milk for your newborn. On the third day after the birth, the breast milk is flowing and your uterus continues to contract. As a new mother, you can become overwhelmed at this point, and there might be tears, worry, and occasionally even feelings of depression. The doctors call this post-partum depression or in laymen's terms it's called "after-baby blues." It's a day not to have visitors scheduled. If possible, it's a great time for Dad to make a point of being home to give you a break, providing tender comfort and strength. Perhaps, your mother or sister can take a turn helping out and relieve your mind of worry. It makes you feel more confident when an experienced woman is around to let you know that **you are doing a wonderful job, and that everything is normal.**

Although your infant is still totally dependent on you and will take up most of your time, her demands are not complicated. Your little one is either hungry, wet, needs to burp, or is tired. She is actually very predictable. When your newborn first wakes up, changing her diaper will make her dry, comfortable, and ready to feed. After breast or bottle-feeding, having taken in a little air with the milk, she is ready to burp. You can put baby over your shoulder with a clean cloth under her chin and pat gently on the back. There is usually a loud satisfied belch that is often accompanied by some spit-up, sometimes even a little flood. Holding your little one in a seated position against your body, facing away from you, with your hands securely under her bum and across her chest is another way to bring up air. If she's finished eating, your satisfied newborn will be ready for some awake time when she will interact with you while observing the world around her. After some play and exercise, it won't be long before she will want to nap. A chance to eat again can soothe her to sleep. If she is fussy, she may enjoy lullabies, a "house tour," or a walk outside. Every three or so hours, you'll repeat these steps.

1. Change diaper
2. Feed
3. Burp
4. Sleep
5. Repeat 1-4

As a new mother, you are instinctively in tune with your baby and ready to feed her when she is hungry. During the nine months that you have been pregnant, the added pressure of the fetus on your bladder caused you to wake up every three hours or so. Your sleep patterns have coincidentally fallen in sync with your baby's feeding schedule, sleeping for about three hours and then waking up to eat. Your breasts will be so full of milk that they can even be dripping, and you are more than ready to nurse when she gives you that hungry cry. The placenta that was nourishing her for nine months has finished its work, and a young digestive system is learning how to handle milk for the first time. Nature is efficiently at work, and the age-old process of nurturing your little one is in balance.

Even at this tender age, she is settling into a routine. *When one of our babies cried, for example, I would pick him up and cuddle him and then change his diaper. Even if he was sucking like crazy, changing his diaper before feeding was an easy habit to establish. It's kind of like washing his hands before dinner when he gets older. Soon he will know the routine, and he'll be dry and comfortable for his feeding. Our son-in-law would make his son laugh with brum, brum and beep, beep car sounds while wearing his T-shirt that said, "Dads who change diapers rock."* Teaching your little one to wait patiently for what he wants creates a calm connection between you.

On the other hand, some parents cannot stand to hear a baby crying. Think of it this way: Without language yet, it's her way of talking to you, saying what she needs, while exercising her lungs at the same time. You can sing to her, tell her it'll be just a moment before mealtime, and that you love her so much. Don't let her cry rattle you. Speak back to her soothingly, she's just trying to talk to you. Soon she will understand that you are competently taking care of business. There's no need to respond in a frantic, hurried, or upset manner. Your secure touch, gentle words, and patient and calm cuddling will settle your baby down and a healthy routine will be established.

A newborn will usually latch on to the breast or bottle like a natural, but sometimes she can have trouble figuring it out. If you are having difficulty with breast-feeding, there are helpful lactation specialists like the La Leche League at www.lllusa.org (in the USA)[61] that have been helping new mothers for sixty years. *Ina May's Guide to Breastfeeding* is a great reference source.[62]

Nursing provides a well-formulated diet, with built-in vitamins and immunities. If you cannot nurse, for whatever reason, bottle-feeding becomes a bonding time too. A quiet place away from the TV, loud music, or large crowds allows baby to comfortably eat her lunch without distractions. Sitting in a rocking chair and lying down in bed were my two favorite nursing positions, where I was totally relaxed and my back was well supported. It's a time to put your whole attention into your little angel. Later, during the family meal, everyone will connect and talk about the happenings of the day. Kids thrive when a healthy routine is created at an early age.

Occasionally, a newborn will cry with a frantic, uncontrollable wail that can worry mom. *When my first child, Brian, was a newborn, we spent an afternoon visiting with friends who wanted to welcome and fuss over him. When I returned home and laid him down, he began to cry, his yell unnervingly desperate and loud. I checked for a wet diaper and then tried to feed him, but Brian was irritable and did not want to nurse. He did not want to be held and yelled when I again tried to lay him down in his crib. I was feeling desperate. What is wrong with my baby? I even checked to see if a diaper pin had come loose and was poking him. (Are there such things these days?) Nothing I did seemed to calm him down. When I picked him up, he cried even louder. I thought, "Oh, no, I have lost my connection with him. Why is he crying so frantically like this? Help!" I finally laid him in his bed and walked outside to take a break. When I came back a few minutes later, he had cried himself into a deep sleep. I then realized what had happened; both of us had become excessively tired and Brian's young nervous system was over-amped. He was wired and tired and my fatigue was reverberating off of him. The more I worried, picked him up and put him down, the more exhausted he became. The yelling actually wore him out and settled him down. Without me around, he was able to fall asleep. That was a real lesson for me. Wet, hungry, gas, or tired, babies are not that complicated.* If you have checked all these things and there is still something wrong, or seems to be, talk to someone who knows about babies.

    Building a support team during your pregnancy becomes an asset when baby arrives. Advice can come from grandmothers, mothers, aunts, or friends who are mothers and have been through it all before. They remember what it was like when they had their first child and worried over every little thing. They know the warning signs for something serious. If your family and friends cannot help, connect with your health care provider. Mothers know to check for fevers, constipation, teething, rashes, and coughs. Your baby receives a certain amount of immunities through the mother's breast milk. Infants are usually born healthy and tough, and generally there is nothing to worry about. However, do what it takes to rest your mind at ease. Your baby feels your worry and uncertainties, as well as your confidence and calm. It never hurts to ask a professional, even if it's only for your own peace of mind. Don't be shy. Sometimes all you need is someone telling you that "you are a good mother," and "your instincts are serving you well." Moms quickly gain the knowledge and intuition of motherhood, and you usually will sense what is best for your little one.

Sometimes something can be upsetting your newborn and you can't figure it out. Certain foods, for instance, can upset a young digestive system. I have a close friend whose baby had such gas pains after nursing that he only slept about an hour at a time. After six weeks both mom and baby were exhausted. A friend gave her a book by Dr. Lendon Smith where he explained that onions, garlic, beans, cabbage, cauliflower, broccoli, spices and even citrus fruits had chemical components that could create gas in babies.[63]

When my friend went on a bland diet, her baby slept for eight hours! She felt such relief to finally find the solution. In any situation, if you are unsure of what is going on, search until you find a satisfactory answer.

Babies love to be sung to and cuddled. There is nothing better than a gentle foot massage, not too light and not too hard, to help a fussy baby fall asleep. It welcomes them to this world, and helps them feel grounded in their physical body. Then again, there are squirmy and fussy babies who are not comfortable being held. A firm hold, however, can sometimes make a difference. It calms her down; she feels protected and secure in your reassuring arms. Swaddling a fussy baby is also an old trick passed down for millennia that works with some infants. Wrap the newborn's body snuggly in a receiving blanket with her arms next to her sides. The tightly wrapped "baby burrito" gives your little one a feeling of being tightly packed in your womb, and they often go right to sleep, settle down to nurse, or peaceably hang out. Also, babies love physical exercise. Run those little legs, and clap those little hands. Roll her gently and slowly over one-way and then the other. Stand your baby up on your lap and see how she pushes off to strengthen her leg muscles. Singing or playing music for your newborn can also be pleasing to her, and she will kick out her feet as if she wants to dance. Keeping the volume down will keep her ears from being damaged. Leave that for a concert in her teenage years. When your baby is awake, just being with her can give you a deep sense of oneness that permeates the bonding. The more you interact with your little one, the more you see her learn and grow, a magical transformation before your eyes. Infants show incredible intelligence. She may not know the words, but she is aware of what you are talking about, your tone, and body language. Speaking to your baby like the bright, sweet, and telepathic person that she is begins a respectful communication that can last a lifetime.

Newborns thrive when they are given lots of loving parental attention. Preemies and other miracle babies in intensive care units have a better chance of survival when there is the touch and caring of mothers and her support crew.

Over four decades ago, when my eldest son Brian was born prematurely, the hospital did not allow me to have contact with him. For three weeks, I viewed my son longingly through the thick glass window of the nursery, while he added on a half ounce at a time in the incubator. I am sure he felt me, but it was not the same as the physical contact that is permitted today. It is well known that a mother's touch is a contributing factor to the overall health of an infant.

A newborn adds a wonderful dimension to your

family. However, you and your partner are the core of the family and may need to take some time to be together, just the two of you. After your little one is born, you are with her day and night, and sometimes you might forget in the hustle and bustle of child-rearing that your relationship could use some space to recharge your batteries. Making time to be alone to relax in each other's love becomes a priority. Not only is this time for you as a couple, but when you get along, your child's emotional health thrives. Can you accept a family member's offer to watch baby for a few hours so you can go out for a nice dinner and a chance to be alone? Children can feel when their security umbrella is content and intact. A happy marriage is a special gift parents can bestow on their children.

Infants

In about five or six months, your baby has become a sociable person. He smiles, recognizing Mom and Dad, and likes to be around other children, especially his older siblings who are role models. The routines of eating, playing and sleeping are set, and you and your baby have developed an understanding of how things work. Your athlete is "scootching," turning over, sitting up, and wanting to crawl. It's amazing how fast he catches on. He smiles, and even attempts to mouth a word or two. Your infant is a keen scientist, carefully observing his world and reaching out to communicate. It's special to be a part of his daily discoveries and explorations. Holding and touching him is satisfying and beneficial to you both.

During the first year of your child's life, you will see his unique personality emerge. He will develop his own temperament, in addition to eating, playing, and sleeping. These habits will be the groundwork for his life, influenced by you and your family. If you can remain calm and keep your sense of humor when he tries out his new repertoire, he will learn what works to get your attention. If you freak out or become frazzled when your infant yells, for instance, eventually he may get in the habit of yelling to get a rise out of you. Certainly, an infant is eager for attention and does not yet distinguish between positive or negative energy. He just knows that he wants it.

Sometimes a baby just can't be consoled, and after you have made sure that you have taken care of all of his basic needs, you can put him in the crib and tenderly tell him that you will come back and pick him up when he stops crying. This practice is basically giving him and maybe more importantly, **you** a short "time-out." You could use a moment to relax for a minute and calm yourself. Removing him from the center of the action will often be just what he needed in the first place. He is probably tired and will fall asleep in a few minutes and the house will return to normal. When he wakes up, he will be cheerful and ready to be part of the family again.

If your baby is still crying after you have taken a short break and a few deep breaths, go talk lovingly to him. If that doesn't settle him down, pick him up to cuddle, sing to him, take a walk around the house, or go outside for some fresh air. With a relaxed outlook, you will be back in tune with your infant and can take care of his needs.

During the first six months of an infant's life, wellness check-ups are scheduled with his doctor or midwife, and there's a calendar for vaccinations. *In my case, with approximately 700 children living closely together on The Farm, we felt that it was important to vaccinate our children with the recommended polio, DPT (diphtheria, tetanus, and whooping cough), measles, mumps, and rubella shots.*

Each summer when I was growing up in Korea, everyone in our community would line up for a smallpox, polio, cholera, typhoid, and DPT shots. These diseases in the 1950's and 60's were not uncommon, killing many people each year and leaving many others with physical deformities and disabilities.

Weaning Your Baby

If you plan to breast feed, there will come a time when baby will eventually cut back on breast milk to two or three times a day. There are mothers, for example, who nurse for six months to a year, and then there are cultures where the mom breastfeeds for two or even three years.

Your child begins the weaning process when he starts eating solid foods and, depending on the child, this can be an easy transition or may pose a challenge. Most kids will gradually lose interest and they easily move on to sitting at the table and eating with the family.

If your child is being slightly disrespectful of the nursing experience, and starts biting your nipple or is too demanding while not listening to your warnings, it is probably a signal that he is getting ready to stop. Many children are attached to nursing and the strong bond to Mama, but a slow withdrawal usually works out fine. If you return to work and leave your little one at day care, the mid-day nursing session will disappear, and if you have breakfast ready, he tends to forget about the morning one too. When solid food gradually takes over, feeding time is still a chance to connect. At bedtime, there can be a book and cuddle time with Mom, or Dad can take a turn putting him to sleep. Usually he will be ready for these changes, and in a few weeks or a few months, he will begin feeding himself. The physical connection that was such a part of nursing doesn't have to disappear; hugs and cuddles are always welcomed.

The Challenging Twos

You often hear parents refer to this period of their child's life as the "terrible twos." These times are exciting, challenging, time-consuming, and humorous, but not terrible. No need to over stress about a totally tidy house for instance; there will be plenty of time for that later. Children are only young for a relatively short time and before you know it, she will be helping you wash the dishes and put the laundry away. At two years old, she has new discoveries and challenges to tackle every day. What an adventure: funny incidents, toys, books, walks, new words, and even sentences! Have you taken that big step into potty training, or is she just getting around to it?

Making your home a safe playground is part of Mom and Dad's job. Anything that is within reach is your explorer's kingdom. Childproofing your home makes things safe since she doesn't know the difference between colorful blocks, the valuable antique vase, or an electrical outlet.

The two-year old's great age of discovery begins as early as a year. As soon as baby has learned to crawl and walk, she can travel to every room in the house, getting into everything within reach. She is an eager scientist of her new world, testing everything with all of her senses. How does this work? What is its name? What noise does it make? Why does it work that way? What does it taste like? Because things go indiscriminately into her mouth - bugs, dirt, and toys - a careful watch is required. On the other hand, pots and pans are tough. She can take them out of the cabinet, play with them, and then you can have her help you put them away. It is a game, but she is already learning that picking up after playtime is what you do, and it encourages her to be mom's little helper.

Your toddler will appreciate a daily routine with

some structure like morning hugs, regular meal times, naps, a walk or a trip to the park, baths, and bedtime. Is she asking nicely for food, washing her hands before eating, and brushing her few new teeth afterwards? While you prepare dinner, can she pick up her toys? Reading a story in the evening settles things down, and she's soon fast asleep. There is security in knowing how her household works. When there's a blip in the routine, explain to her what is going to happen, and she can settle easily into the new adventure.

After a romp in the park, or a play date with a friend, she will usually look forward to a nap. Giving a toddler caffeinated soft drinks or heavily sugared or processed foods can make it almost impossible for her to relax. Screen time also can be a stimulant and prevent your young child from nodding off. If she becomes cranky and intolerable, she probably needs a rest. Soon, new mothers become aware of their child's routines and anticipate their needs. Mellow activities, like reading a story or singing songs, will usually settle a child down. Let your two-year old know how lucky she is to take a break and invite her to lie down with you and share your nice, warm bed. They are such sweeties when they have enough sleep.

Kids are talented impersonators, miming the speech, attitudes, and body language of the people nearby. They can be great mirrors for a parent, showing you what you look like in ways that you might not have noticed. A toddler can pick up a habit and parade it around, often making you laugh or maybe cry when you realize where she learned that one. When you see your perfect little angel copying some of your less than exemplary behavior, it can inspire you to make some changes. It's possible to eliminate your negative mannerisms, and they will most likely fade away from your young child's repertoire. When you drop old patterns, you will become more confident and decisive. If you and your kid evolve together, there will be less hypocrisy in the relationship and more camaraderie. Parents are not infallible, but if you are honest and believable, your children will trust you.

It might come as a surprise when your child imitates you or your partner's behavior. For example, if Dad occasionally yells at Mom, it is not long before your child will occasionally yell at Mom too. Your toddler sees that this is acceptable behavior. Unfortunately, Mom now has to contend with two people giving her a hard time. She obviously needs to stand up for herself and insist that everyone treat her nicely. What is Dad's problem? Whatever it is, let's address the issue so the shouting stops. That is what Mom really wants. When parents show respect for each other, the children learn to be respectful. Suppose Mom does not stand up for herself? She will build up resentment and repressed anger. At some point, she starts screaming too and jumps into the fray. The family has now forged an agreement that allows everyone to participate in unkind, disrespectful behavior. After a while, it becomes the norm and the parents may stop noticing it, but the children cringe in fear when the yelling begins. It isn't always this glaringly obnoxious, but there can be bickering, sarcastic slights, and jabs that any outside observer notices immediately. A counselor or trusted friend can see these subconscious family agreements and provide insights into understanding the root causes. After working it through, peace can then return to the home.

It's one thing to have a disagreement with Dad and quite another to get into an argument with a young child. Your youngster doesn't have reasoning skills yet, and is just beginning to learn about limits, rules, and acceptable behavior. The parents are in charge and set down understandable boundaries within the household. A family is not a democracy! Being consistent and firm about upholding your agreements keeps everything running smoothly.

Potty-Training

When it comes to potty training, some children adapt easily to the routine while others catch on a little later. How do you know when your child is ready? You might inspire her with a potty chair placed next to Mom and Dad's toilet. There are engaging books about potty training that can become her favorites such as *Potty Time!* by Caroline Jayne Church and *Everyone Poops* by Taro Gomi.[64]

If you are uninhibited enough when you go to the bathroom, have her sit on her pot nearby and go together. You can also invite her to sit on the pot every hour or so to get her used to it. If your child has a habit of pooping at the same time each day, having her sit on the potty at that time often yields good results. Giving her encouraging words when she pees or poops in the potty supports her progress. Some kids enjoy putting stickers on a chart. Positive reinforcement is the name of the game, and there is no need for any pressure.

Have faith, stay unattached, and eventually the potty thing becomes a habit. If you feel any resistance, stop for a while before trying again. Parents who demand performance can end up with a rebellious two-year-old exercising "pee power" or "poop power." You may be tired of changing diapers, or worry that your child is behind her peers, but any pressure on your part can result in a tug-of-war power struggle. If your child refuses to use the potty, don't stress. She will want to be a "big kid," like her friends, soon enough.

Babysitting

When our children were toddlers, I started working part-time and brought them over to our neighborhood-babysitting group. Having a few days of the week to be with other adults was great for my state of mind. I was able to be productive in my flextime job, and came home with renewed enthusiasm for my family. I felt secure that caring moms were watching my children, and the kids had fun playing with their pals.

When I brought one of my sons to the babysitters for the first time, he put up a big fuss, and I felt like the meanest mom in the world, abandoning him to these horrible strangers (our familiar next-door-neighbors.) I hugged him and told him that I would be back soon. After an interesting morning's work, I returned to pick him up, and the other mothers told me how sweet he had been as soon as I walked out of sight. After that, things became routine and I didn't worry.

Because families are often dependent on two incomes, day care or a babysitter often comes into the picture. If you have family that can help you cover the kids, count yourself as one of the lucky ones. Taking your child to day care for the first few times may be traumatic for you or your toddler. Do you like the way the caretakers handle her? Can you have friendly and honest discussions about how she is doing? These support people are your partners in parenting, and it helps to bounce things off of them; it can relieve mom's babysitting anxiety. If there is something about the situation that feels wrong or worrisome, can you discuss this with the babysitter or day care provider? If you, or your child continues to be uncomfortable, consider trying out another baby-sitting option.

Remember that your intuitive or gut feeling is your warning signal that something is not right. For example, our 1 ½ year old grandson was not having a good time at a day care when our daughter was working on her master's degree. She asked us if we could give her a month of Nana/Baba time so she could finish up her thesis before her second child was due. It turned into a win-win situation since we had a great time taking our grandson out each day; he loved being with us, and his mom was able to do her work in peace. When family can step in to help with child-care, everyone benefits.

Discipline

When it comes to disciplining your child, your two-year old tyke does not understand that there might be a difference between good and bad manners, or polite and impolite behavior. Morals and values are not preprogrammed, and it's up to you to show her how life works in an age appropriate way. It might seem that she is breaking every rule in the book. However, if you give her reasonable and accurate feedback, you teach your two-year old about *cause and effect, avoiding danger, and personal responsibility*. Testing her limits is what a two-year old does, and your job is to show her that certain boundaries and limits exist. When she does something hurtful, harmful or reckless, there are consequences. If you aren't careful, you'll find yourself saying No, No, No, Don't do that, Don't, Don't, Don't. Is it any wonder that "no" often becomes a toddler's favorite word?

Teenagers and toddlers have some things in common. They are both rounding a corner and testing their limits. How much independence can I have? How far will my parents let me go? If you magnify your two-year old child's behavior into a fifteen-year old body, what does it look like? If it is no big deal, then let it go. If it looks like a monster, keep calm and proceed decisively. Having humor, patience, and unconditional love handy at all times makes life easier. Your toddler is easily distracted and you can redirect her into a fun activity. If she is on a tantrum, it is much easier to discipline your little rascal now, when you can pick her up like a football under your arm and carry her off to the crib for a couple of minutes of time-out. When you take care of business consistently at this age, you will have a better chance of success when she becomes a teenager.

Children feel secure when they have boundaries. If they are acting up, they may be tired or hungry or they may be asking for limits. They are testing their world while you are honing your child-raising skills. If you make a mistake, they will forgive you; telling your two-year-old you are sorry shows her how to apologize. After you have set limits, she will test them again and again to make sure you were serious the first and second and third time. Be original, be funny, and be wilder and crazier than she is. When you give her a different response and vary your tone, you won't be saying the same thing over and over again. That would be boring for both of you, wouldn't it?

What can you do when your child acts up, goes on a tantrum, or in general causes havoc, especially out in public? Everyone has seen a young child who is kicking and screaming, being totally outrageous while her mother is saying very softly and sweetly, "Now dear, that is not being very nice. Please, Mommy would like you to stop crying." Hey! Mom! Your child can't hear you above her own noise! When this happens in a public place, remove her from the action as quickly as possible, since her antics are attracting undue attention while she feeds off of the spotlight. Be quick but not angry that your little angel has interrupted your shopping trip. Besides, a two-year-old needs age-appropriate activities to ensure fun for both of you. She can be a good shopper especially when she is asleep in her stroller, but if she is tired and grouchy, maybe not. The 'gimmes' take over and a royal fit can erupt over candy or potato chips. When you are planning to go out, make it short and interesting. You might offer her a choice of one item that she will receive at the end of the trip. When she is rested and up for the shopping adventure, she likes riding in the cart, and you'll both have an enjoyable time. If you need to go on a larger grocery run or you want to shop for yourself, can you find someone to baby-sit or wait until your partner can take a turn? Your toddler will have more fun at home or playing in the park with other children, while you take needed time off for yourself. It won't be long before she will get a thrill out of helping you pick out the groceries.

Occasionally behaving outrageously is something that toddlers do. Is she used to getting what she wants? Is there a big fuss if she doesn't? Did she grab a toy away from her friend or hit someone? Or did a child grab a toy away from her? Can you ask what happened? If you can find out what caused the upset and make it right, the play can continue and this incident becomes a chance to show what sharing is all about. But if nothing is working, removing your child from the action is the usual, easy discipline; she has earned herself a time-out. Keep anger and frustration out of your voice and words. Are the crib rails high enough so she can't climb out? After your toddler has been placed in the crib, let her know why she is there and that she can come play when she settles down. When she stops the temper tantrum and calms down, you might be able to find out what upset her and reasonably talk it out and make things fair. It is not long before she learns what leads to a time out and also how to regain her freedom. She will soon grasp the idea that in order to be a part of the action, she will need to be civil. You will know when your toddler is ready to return to play when she stops howling, grabbing, hitting, or whatever it was. If she has hurt someone, learning to say, "I am sorry" helps repair the damage. Or she can give a warm hug to someone she has mistreated.

Keeping your wits about you can be difficult when you are going through this process. When you are disciplining your child, are you still speaking nicely, even if it is firmly and at a higher volume? It's easy to lose your patience and have anger and frustration take over. Resist the urge!

Kids respond respectfully when they are treated like intelligent human beings. Are you speaking to your child in a high-pitched baby voice? You wouldn't feel too happy if the tables were reversed and you were not taken seriously. With their sharp awareness, they understand their new world on many levels, picking up the nuances of what you are saying, which includes approval, disappointment, guilt, and frustration. When you treat her like you'd like to be treated, hearing what she is trying to say, good communication skills will become part of your family routine.

Unfortunately, there are parents who are overly strict and sometimes downright mean. There are also parents who do not give their children enough attention and are negligent. And then there are those parents who, in trying to do their best, are too permissive and lenient. A two-year-old thrives on good attention, and not only during the fun times. You are giving her the fundamentals of how to fit into her family and society through your interactions. Spending quality time together usually results in less "time-outs" and, later on, fewer calls from the principal's office. If she does not receive the guidelines now, there will undoubtedly be harsher measures later on. The cold shower at age 12 or 13 awaits. We have all seen teens and adults who weren't taught the basics of sharing, kindness, and respect for others, not to mention for themselves.

There are rare times in the life of a young child when it becomes necessary to give her important life and death lessons. For example, if your child runs out into the street chasing a ball, the worst thing possible could happen. Mom is totally freaked out that her child was in mortal danger. Her continuous verbal warnings were so blatantly and dangerously disregarded that it could have been a real disaster. It's time for action, and it must be now. Choose your discipline and make sure your child understands the ramifications of what she has done. Later, ideally when Dad is around, it's time for a serious talk. Hopefully, this gets your child's attention about the significance of the situation and she will understand the boundaries and consequences from an early age. She will begin to recognize the tone in your voice that you are serious and will listen to you.

After it is all said and done, make sure that she understands that she cannot run into the street, for instance, because cars are dangerous. Did she get it? Have her look you in the eyes and respectfully acknowledge what you said. Then give her a warm hug and tell her that you are glad that she is listening because you love her so much and don't want her to get hurt.

It is a touchy subject about spanking, hitting, or slapping. A few generations ago it was the common form of discipline. The switch or paddle was used at home and even by teachers and principals at school. When I was raising my children, I still believed there were times when a spanking was needed, when it was a dangerous situation that was blatantly disregarded, there was a just cause. We tried to refrain from that form of discipline except in the most serious cases. Spankings could only be given by a biological parent and never in anger. However, my children have taken it a step further, and never condone spanking. Physical force is a violent action that instills fear and they do not believe in violence against their children. I respect this new way of treating children and other methods that are working well, and am glad that we can move forward into a non-violent way of dealing with our children.

When you and your partner are consistent about upholding the boundaries and dealing out discipline when your child crosses the line, she will know that her life will be safe when she follows your lead and listens to what you say. The consequences, depending on the seriousness of the offense, can be in the firmness of your voice, (not angry but firm), her removal from the center of the action, or denying something that she wants. However, kids often test their boundaries, and you'll need to be on your toes to make sure the limits are followed with consistency. When you treat each other with respect, there will be less defiance and the need for repercussions.

When parents are in agreement about a situation and how they will deal with it, it makes a huge difference. If one of you is too soft and one is too authoritarian, the child will try to work one of you against the other. If the situation happens again, and you show the same unified message, children will soon get the idea. Two of my favorite books about raising kids are Faber and Mazlish's, *How to Talk to Kids So Kids Will Listen and Listen So Kids Will Talk*[65] and Gary Chapman and Ross Campbell's *The Five Love Languages for Children.*[66]

The early years are crucial in forming your unique and precious child's future habits, allowing her personality to develop and shine. Spending quality time with your toddler can make a huge difference in her life. If you can tighten the economic belt or work part time in order to stay home with your young children for a few years, it will be worth it in the long run.

Screen Time

When I wrote this book over two decades ago, there were no smart phones and screen time referred to hours spent in front of a television or a computer, not a gadget that you could have at your fingertips constantly. Even back in the 1970's people were alarmed about children watching too much TV and especially shows depicting excessive violence and foul language. Most television stations signed off the air at midnight and there were only three major channels. After cable came along the numerous channels ran 24 hours a day every day. There are homes where the TV is on all the time; call it background noise, white noise, or a babysitter.

On The Farm, we lived without electricity for years. We had kerosene lanterns and a party-line phone system with an operator for long distance calls. When we began to have electricity, we ran on trickle charge batteries, so we had limited power and might watch a show like Saturday Night Live or the sit-com, Soap, once a week. A World Series or Super Bowl ball game would attract many people huddled around a small, black and white TV.

After we moved to California, we eventually bought a TV. The young children enjoyed Sesame Street and the Saturday morning cartoons were a treat. As the kids grew into their teens, we would watch a movie, a game, nature programs, and MTV. These days when we live on our sailboat in Mexico for six months each year, we totally unplug from TV, radio, and movies. When we are within cell phone range we can access our mail and the Internet. We are able to pull down weather reports that tell us when it is safe to go out sailing and when it would be prudent to stay at anchor. We have Single Side Band and HAM radio nets each day (old technology) and many of our cruising friends have Sirius Radio, SAT phones, and Garmin InReach Explorer,[67] a Satellite Communicator, and GPS Tracking Devise. If something is especially important, we do hear about it.

When we return to civilization, we get back into our gadgets, with a look at the news, and watch Jeopardy, the great wild life shows, and an occasional professional sports program. We also watch movies that were recommended by friends who said, "You must see this one." After six months at home, we appreciate our vacation from screen time, immersing ourselves again into a real life Discovery Channel Nature Show.

There are plenty of good things to be said about our many gadgets that keep us up on the latest news around the globe, and innovative programs that explore our world and the many amazing animals, plants, weather systems, outer space, and ways humans are working to repair damage to our environment. There are history and science programs that visually fill in gaps in our knowledge about everything. Social media brings our far-flung families together, sharing pictures, activities, and ideas. There are amazing children's programs and apps that teach interactive math, reading, and science. And, there's probably a zillion things whizzing by me that I'll never know anything about.

Nowadays, we don't necessarily want to totally unplug, although it's a wonderful thing to do from time to time, to leave your cell phone at home and go out on a nature walk, leaving all the chatter behind. However, there have been warnings that excessive screen time can be detrimental to a person's physical and mental health. It can take the place of exercise and social time with friends. There are warnings about it harming the retina of the eye, not to mention the rise in obesity, and an increase in mood swings, suicide, depression, and insomnia. The screen's rapid shifting from picture to picture is apparently contributing to hyperactivity. It's like candy and can be highly addictive. A parent's responsibility is to monitor the time their child spends in front of a screen and make it safe for them. The latest studies say that a child younger than 5th grade should not have more than an hour of screen time a day. Two hours is more than enough for older children, and they can then spend time in imaginative play with friends, reading books, and playing sports.[68]

      The trick is to not turn screen time into a battle, but to decide how much is healthy, and then remove the phone or shut off the TV when the time is up. There are apps that block and filter usage. Watching a special program with your child can be an extra treat. Our world is rapidly changing on the technology front and parents are stepping up to create the boundaries in their homes that are good for them and their children.

Learning Disabilities

Some of our most famous scientists, successful businessmen, and leaders had learning disabilities and experienced difficulties in the traditional school system. However, they learned to compensate and went on to find success. If you are wondering if your child has a learning disability, there are evaluations to determine how she is doing. Most children will be in the normal range, and the parents will be relieved. However, there are a certain number of children who have special needs. If they are able to work with trained teachers, they can succeed in school and live a happy life. Early intervention usually makes a big difference. The sooner you start implementing innovative approaches to learning, the better your child's chances are of reaching her potential.[69]

Sometimes learning disabilities don't show up until the child begins school, and she has trouble keeping up with her peers. When this happens, working together with her teacher, who has seen it before, can lead to finding creative ways of grasping knowledge. Two and a half million students in the U.S. have learning disabilities, with only 41% of these students receiving special educational services. 75% - 80% of the disabilities are in language and reading, with the result that 60% of adults with severe literacy problems have an undetected or untreated learning disability.[70]

Your child has important talents to share and a valuable place in the future of his/her world. www.ldonline.org/profbooks/c687 offers books that can help you with your child's specific learning disability.

Children have various ways to learn, through their eyes, by hearing, or by kinetic learning, which is more hands on. Often kids with learning disabilities are just as intelligent as their peers, but their brains are simply wired differently and they may not thrive in the structure of our school system.[71]

Also, 33% of kids with learning disabilities are gifted. They can have difficulty with reading, writing, speaking, spelling, or math, but might be great at coding, robot building, art, or music. Or, possibly there might be a problem that affects an individual's attention, memory, social skills, or emotional maturity. Behavioral modification therapy techniques have proven helpful. Also, seeking a counselor will hook you up with a support group, and your child can receive the appropriate guidance. You can access services and programs to put you in touch with what you need. Being in contact with other parents who have children with learning disabilities gives you added knowledge and support.

The Preschool Years
(3 to 5 years)

Kids are constantly going through different phases. There are times when your child is sweet, helpful, and easygoing as can be, and then, turns into a little terror on other days. During these good times, everyone understands each other. He becomes a whiz at counting, saying the ABC's, and playing with other children. When you talk together, he begins to understand the whys and how's of things, and a life-long dialogue has begun. When grandma comes to visit, she is impressed with his vocabulary and how he said "Thank you" when he received a gift. If he is having a rough day, letting him air his feelings, with you listening and being there for him, encourages him to weather out his problems and come out the other side.

Your child is coming into his own awareness. He has definite opinions about what he likes, what to wear, and what to eat. It can be easy to find yourself in a tug of war over anything so it's advisable to pick your battles wisely. If he wants to wear a red cape or fireman's outfit, more power to him. If he likes celery stuffed with peanut butter or spaghetti with your famous sauce, fine. Some kids are happy with the same meal of rice and tofu, or beans and tortillas as long as you add some carrot sticks or broccoli to encourage vegetables in his diet. Whatever it is, as long as it is somewhat healthy, let's not make a big deal about it. Encourage him to take a taste of everything. He might find that it is surprisingly yummy, just like Sam I Am discovered in Dr. Seuss's *Green Eggs and Ham*.[72]

Giving him control of some of his life choices is part of growing up.

Then there are times when you teach him limits and boundaries and hold your ground. Saying "good morning" or "hello" for example, when someone greets him is a basic courtesy that will serve him well for a lifetime. Is he kind to other kids? Does he share? Does he do what you ask without grumbling? Is the household running relatively smoothly? There is a delicate balance between allowing him to be himself and in control of his choices and setting boundaries to teach him how to relate with others as well as keep him safe.

It can be a major transition when your child enters preschool, especially if he hasn't already spent some time in a day care setting. Depending on how your child adapts, easing him in for one or two days a week allows him to get used to this new routine while being away from Mama. At preschool, he learns to interact with an adult who is not his parent, and has the opportunity to mix it up with his peers. Also, having play dates when he is young will help him learn the basics of interacting with other kids. He learns to share while getting used to the idea of not being the center of attention. When you are in close communication with the preschool staff, you can let them know if your child is unusually shy or overly rambunctious, for instance, and they can bring him added assurance and attention.

This may be a time in your young preschooler's life when a new brother or sister is welcomed into the household. These significant changes make for an exciting, and maybe even a disturbing time. When you let your child touch your belly and talk about your pregnancy, making him feel a part of what's going on, it will be easier when the baby arrives.

Our daughter had a great idea when she was pregnant with her second child. She had big brother pick out a gift to wrap for the new baby. He, in turn, received a gift from his new little sister when she was born.

A new baby requires Mom's attention and Daddy's too, attention that your first-born child used to have totally for himself. Who is this interloper? She is cute even though she yells sometimes. Now your preschooler has a real live baby to take care of and likes being Mama's little helper: picking out baby's outfit, bringing a clean diaper, and finding toys for baby to play with. Also, Dad's connection with his oldest child is enhanced when "just the guys" go to the store for needed supplies or do the dishes together, and then go for an outing to the park. There can also be play dates with his friends and relatives, while Mom has bonding time with the new baby. Having your child help you with the newborn makes him feel important, a big boy, and a contributing member to your recently enlarged family. Setting aside time to give him individual attention makes his day.

Balancing family and work is the challenge for this stage of life. Parents of preschool-age children may be offered promotions in their careers or perhaps their business is taking off. When you keep your priorities straight and don't allow work to be more important than your family, your children will appreciate the time you spend with them. Your preschooler thrives on your attention so finding a happy medium is the key, between spending long hours at work and having enough time for your family. Is it possible to arrange your hours at work so that you can spend quality time at home?

With the inevitable 'always somethings' and a tightening schedule, carving out time for date nights with your mate is as important as ever. Your parents, siblings or friends who live nearby are usually more than happy to watch your children and give you a needed break. Taking a family walk after work with the baby in a stroller gives you time to talk out your day. Making love makes the sleep you so desperately need even more restful. It's amazing how time spent with your partner will renew your energy. You may not see each other as much as you would like, but it's great to know that you are in love and are working together to support your growing family. It's about to get even better. You will have moved beyond the diaper and potty training stage, and there will be more opportunities to enhance your first priority, a close relationship with your partner.

The Elementary School Years

When children enter elementary school, they become more aware of who they are in the world apart from their families. Kids this age are comfortable with a regular routine: breakfast, school, homework, chores, dinner, and the bedtime schedule of bath, teeth brushing, and story time. The happy family chugging along is satisfying for everyone.

The student is eager to learn and delves deep into the subjects that interest him. He is excited about tornados and hurricanes, animals and volcanoes, and dinosaurs and carnivorous plants. Big trucks and fire engines, garbage trucks and trains fascinate him, and he begins to pick out books about these things. He also loves it when you read to him. Creating a store, a box full of dress up clothes, or a tunnel made of large cardboard boxes keeps his attention for hours. He is enthralled with building things out of blocks, Legos or Lincoln Logs. His imagination takes him on interesting adventures. He loves nature and wildlife, drawing, puzzles, books, and music. Going on frequent trips to the local library, museum, or zoo encourages his interest in science, reading, writing, and math. Exploring these subjects with your youngster enlivens your own sense of discovery. The Internet is such a great tool when you can look up the question at hand and add facts and pictures to your student's growing knowledge.

He is becoming aware of the outside world and how it works. His fascination with money can turn into earning some for that special item on his wish list. An extra dollar for certain jobs can give him impetus to help out beyond his usual chores. Having a piggy bank and savings account will make him mindful of finances and the different values of bills and coins.

When parents are involved with their kid's education, their youngster usually flourishes. It can be exciting and gratifying to attend soccer games, school conferences, or special events. A parent-teacher conference lets you compare notes and work together with your child's instructor who is in effect your partner in parenting. S/he is with him every weekday and can give an objective look on how well your child is doing. S/he can alert you if there is something that you can do to help him with his learning or social interactions. You can also share any issues from home that might impact your child's progress at school. This will help his teacher be more sensitive to his needs. Working together, you can come up with helpful ways to inspire your child to have a positive experience.

What expectations do you have for your children? Whatever they are, your child will probably not do exactly what you have in mind. Elementary school children have their own wills and interests. It is wonderful to see them develop their individual creative expressions, whatever they might be. During the summer vacation for example, you can help your child decide what activities he wants to do. Most neighborhoods offer swimming classes, science camps, music, art, and sports lessons of all kinds. Allowing him to pick out a few activities he is interested in gives him a choice in the matter, and he's likely to enjoy them.

Generally your days go along in a regular routine of school, work, and weekends. There will be times when things flow along easily, and then you might hit a patch of ice on the road, where your elementary school kid may become willful and not want to do what you ask. He may become glum or angry, or not want to participate in family activities. What do you do when this happens? Can you ask what is bothering him? When the door is open for him to discuss his feelings, he can easily respond with his side of the story, and together you can explore imaginative ways to make the situation better. Is there something at school that he is struggling with? Is there a classmate who makes him uncomfortable? A teacher who was not fair, or something at home that he doesn't like? When he is able to talk things out, reason with you and then come up with solutions to the problem, his mind will be eased and he will be back to being his fun self again.

There has been a swing away from the strict upbringings that many children had in the past and in some ways might be becoming too permissive. Parents may unconsciously give over the parental role to their child and allow him to run the show. Can we call this the "Whatever you want, dear" syndrome? This can backfire when the child flounders in an adult role far above his maturity level, and he will feel insecure with the added responsibility. Your child may act out and you might come up against stubbornness, sassiness, unkindness, disrespect, or bossiness. If the boundaries are fair, age-appropriate, and make sense, he will usually work happily within them. If there's a disagreement between you and your partner, your child might fall into that gap and work one parent against the other to get his way. It's time for the parents to put their heads together, figure out how this happened, take back the parental role, and put the family back into balance. With a unified agreement, sorting out these issues becomes much easier.

When you include your child in the running of the household, he will feel like a contributing member of the family. Hopefully, it won't be a big deal for him to help with chores. Since he was little, you've allowed him to make choices such as what clothes to wear, what games to play, and what special treat to have. However, sometimes you need him to do something where there is no choice in the matter, like chores that need to be done, an appointment that needs to be kept, or he needs to stop terrorizing his younger sibling. And then there are mornings when he has to get himself together in time for school. And, while he's at it, can he be respectful to his mom and stop the pouting or defiant attitude? When you take a moment to explain why and what you need, he will appreciate being part of the discussion. You might balance a task that needs doing with equal time to play his favorite game or do a fun project together. When it is understood that there are things that are not negotiable, while allowing him to have input on details where he *can* have a choice, your home life usually settles down and your child is happier.

Your growing child seems to have endless energy, and tends to run hard all day nonstop. He may not realize that he needs a snack, some downtime, or a break from the hectic pace of activities and schedules. After school or during the summer, it's nice to have quiet time to read and relax with no appointments to keep.

Children thrive when they show a grasp of a few basic manners that make it so people like having them around, whether it's in a classroom setting or at a friend's home. Part of the parent's job description of raising children is teaching an attitude of respect, which shows up in actions like being considerate and grateful, and answering politely when spoken to. These are basic social graces that parents can teach, especially by practicing them! A great quote from our grandson's marital arts class is: **Attitude is contagious. Is yours worth catching?**[73]

This may be a time to again discuss with your child how actions have consequences. When you are kind, helpful, and truthful, pleasant things happen to you. When you are moody and unfriendly, you'll receive that kind of treatment in return. When something comes up that he thinks is unfair, for example, it becomes an opportunity to learn about life and how to manage the ups and downs in the larger world.

If you rarely involve yourself in your child's activities, is it any wonder that it affects his self-esteem? If you do not find the time to give him positive attention, then he will look elsewhere. One way or another, your child will find the attention that he needs. He will usually settle for any attention offered, whether it is from good role models or peers who might also have low self-esteem and are involved in rebellious behavior. Without care, attention, and guidance, a child is alone on a difficult and hazardous journey.

In our ever-evolving workplace, more mothers than ever have full time jobs. When both parents are working, they reconnect in the evenings to cook dinner, manage the household, and find time to talk out the day's triumphs and problems. It makes a big difference when both Mom and Dad take an active role and share the load. Your children will not only feel covered, but also they will learn about their world from two different points of view, both of which are valuable. When one parent can be at home when their kids return from school, not only when they are little, but even into junior and senior high school, they provide an anchor in the child's life. It is understandable that it is often the bottom line that prevents this from happening. If there is a possibility of living more frugally, changing schedules, having a relative or friend cover you for a few hours, or possibly working at home, it will pay off in the future.

When our daughter's family has the evening meal together, they will often go around the table and each person will say what their high and low event of the day was. This is a great way to share what happened during the day, and can lead to further discussion on how things are going. One grandchild likes to go around the table and hear what each person is thankful for that brings up the highlights of the day.

Being involved with your child does not mean pushing him to do activities to such a degree that he has no time for his own imaginative play. In today's world, we see a child's after-school schedule filled with piano, dance, karate, and soccer resulting in both the parents and kids frazzled from lack of downtime. Creating a balance for your family that includes both quality and quantity time spent with each other is as important as all the jobs and classes.

Kids need challenges and a chance to spread their wings. There will be some boundaries and routines, but these are minor compared to having quality time with you. Outdoor activities and sports are great ways to interact. Reading, arithmetic, history, geography, and science can be fun too when they are intertwined with everyday play and work. These formative years establish good study and work habits. When you are involved, he feels your encouragement and support.

Giving a child freedom to become who he wants to be, - fulfilling his own purpose and following his passion - is part of taking care of your child. Sometimes a parent can become overbearing and controlling, which prevents the child from trying new things on his own, making mistakes, and being an independent thinker. Kids will learn all that they need and want to know over their lifetimes. Allowing him time to pursue what he likes to do, reading a book or having unsupervised play without obligations or schedules, can bring balance to his life.

The amount of positive attention you give your child is directly proportional to his success and happiness. If young people are happy and confident in knowing who they are, they in turn can have positive influences on their peers. Joining a team or club, and taking classes that the child is interested in, allows him to relate to other kids in positive ways. Their friends are involved in activities like they are, and they feed off the excitement of each other's goals and successes. They have friendly rivalries about grades or sports and help each other with school projects. Your child is growing up with his own personality and style, and it's exciting to see him follow his interests. You might wonder where all this will lead.

Middle School

These 11 to 12 year olds who were the top dogs at their elementary school are making a transition into a new level when they enter Junior High School. They are navigating their world of school, siblings, and friendships, and have an idea of who they are and what interests them.

Practically overnight, your child's homework is starting to challenge your brain. She is involved in activities where she is both proficient and passionate. Her world has expanded. Perhaps she has traveled to interesting places, helped Dad with one of his house projects, performed in a school play, participated in competitive sports, and, in general, tasted a sampling of what life has to offer.

Introducing your pre-teen to new experiences broadens her world and makes life intriguing. Encouraging hobbies and doing projects together can be happy times for both of you. Camping, sporting events, music programs, art shows, and participating in community service projects (like filling boxes of food for the homeless or visiting an elderly relative or friend) give her a varied smorgasbord of life's possibilities. Soon enough, she would rather be with friends than with parents, but at this age, she still appreciates your involvement with her extra curricular activities. When you attend her athletic games, theater productions, or whatever, you give your child positive affirmation. Creating a welcoming home where she and her buddies can come hang out, have a snack, play music, or do homework together will keep you connected. Your maturing child is now old enough to go off to camp, visit a relative who lives further away, and go to sleepovers with friends. When parents encourage this independence, your child experiences the real world and begins to formulate her own belief systems, ideas, and points of view. When the family gets together, her original opinions will enliven the conversation.

Your child is growing up, not only in her way of thinking, but physically and emotionally, and it all seems to be happening at once. Her maturity and depth of insight might surprise you one minute, while in the next she will feel unsure of herself. Physically your pre-teen can feel gawky or gangly; she doesn't feel as beautiful as all of the models and pop stars in the ubiquitous media. Those braces to straighten her teeth might make her feel unattractive, but at least she has the option to order them in pretty colors. Giving her compliments and treating her with tenderness will go a long way towards building her self-esteem and making this transitional age a fun and exciting adventure.

Physically, the pre-teens are changing rapidly from children to adults. Girls will start their periods; their bodies are changing, with breasts beginning to develop, hair growing in various places, and estrogen hormones alternating with progesterone are pulsing. Boys' voices begin to crack and drop into the lower octaves, hair begins to grow on their faces and elsewhere, and testosterone hormones are racing through their veins.[74]

Explosively happy and then angry emotions can surface, erupting without warning, or they can be deeply hidden as your evolving child retreats, learning how to cope with life. If you ask her the usual questions of "How was your day?" or "What did you do in school?" you may get that age old response like "Okay" or "Nothing much." These sullen moods seem to say, "Keep out of my business and my life," which leaves you feeling rejected, angry, or helpless. How are you going to respond, when for all these years, you've been encouraging your child to be respectful and cheerful?

You may even feel like your parenting job is coming to an end. However, for the next ten years (whether your kid thinks so or not), your presence in her life as a mentor, cheerleader, role model, and guide is more important than ever. She may not acknowledge it, but she is watching you. It might seem like she has stopped listening, but she is taking what you say to heart, and reworking it to fit her needs. There may be a push and pull while she moves towards adulthood, and you can let go, freeing her to discover her own path. Your child will be looking for your unconditional love and support even when it seems like she would rather be with friends. She will probably do things differently than you did, and may challenge some of your values and beliefs. When you stand by and love her unconditionally, you will be her support when she negotiates through this amazing transition.

Partnering with your child's teachers makes a big difference. Kudos to the brave teachers everywhere! They teach your kids five days a week, challenging them to live up to their potential while beginning to prepare them for life on their own. These dedicated men and women are heroes. They create a protective bubble around your children that allows them to grow intellectually, physically, and emotionally in a stimulating learning environment. These teachers arrive every day ready to teach, not knowing which kids will be up or down, enthusiastic or uninterested, had a bad day at home, or just broke up with their first true love.

To navigate through these few years will stretch you in ways you never imagined while, hopefully, strengthening the bonds that last a lifetime.

A Family Meeting

When your child reaches this age of reason, she begins to play an important part in family affairs, sharing her opinions and ideas. With everyone's busy schedules, it helps to have a forum where things can be openly discussed and each person can have their say. You can create a supportive bubble around the family, where plans are discussed and problems resolved, and each member feels included and responsible to the whole group. Gathering together to talk from time to time clears up issues that are floating around and causing bad feelings. Meetings can begin with a quiet time when each of you tries to relax and become centered. Entering this kind of discussion in a receptive and mellow mood makes it more likely that problems will work out to everyone's satisfaction. Do you need a "talking stick," an item that you pass around to signal that the person holding it speaks without being interrupted? If there is a conflict, she speaks directly to the group about what is happening instead of to the person with whom she is having a problem. When the entire group has respect for the process, there is a good chance that problems can be resolved with insightful wisdom, compassion, and a dash of humor. If a format for running a meeting is needed to solve a nagging problem, there are excellent, group conflict-resolution guidelines found on the Internet.[75]

Why wait until relationships are on the rocks before asking for help? If the family has trouble sorting things out, counseling can be a rewarding way to pursue family growth.

We kept our house clean on the vibrational level with our family meetings that became an essential part of our household, especially when there were disagreements. Problems were talked about and each person had their say. You can always feel if there is an elephant in the room: some big, uncomfortable thing that needs to be talked about. Once we sorted things out and made new agreements, it was time to celebrate and enjoy relaxed family time.

There are ways to stay connected that can create a supportive bubble around the family where problems are resolved and each member feels included and responsible to the whole. Holding a meeting from time to time clears up issues that are floating around causing bad feelings.

The Teenage Years

A teenager is moving rapidly into the big world of his own making, eager to follow his purpose and passion wherever it may lead. Looking back over the years, I can't help but marvel at how that small child who once loved to snuggle while I read to him on the couch is now taller than me, driving a car, and making his own decisions. Having eight children has shown me how unique and different each person from the same family can be. We raised our kids as individuals, encouraging their own natural talents. They had varied interests, confidence about who they are, and were respected for their integrity.

Inevitably, the parent-child connection is fading away while the adult-to-adult relationship is being established. Teenagers experience major changes and discoveries at this transitional time in their lives. He is now more of an adult than a child. He dips his toes in the river, wades in slowly, and eventually swims across to the interesting, sometimes challenging, but always exciting experience of commanding his own life. Still, he often returns to the emotionally secure side of his childhood and family, only to build up his nerve for another foray into adulthood.

Parents make adjustments too. While teens exercise their independence, they still rely on you for most of their financial and emotional support. He is learning how to make choices and decisions on his own, and you continue to show him how an adult takes responsibility for himself and the family. If you are his confidant during this transition time, it makes things easier. It's nice when you can invite his teen buddies over to the house for meals and games. Hopefully, he chooses to run with a reasonably responsible and respectful crowd and when he goes out with friends, you'll have no problem trusting the group to have a safe, fun time (Keep your fingers crossed and knock on wood). Teens may tell you that they don't appreciate having well-defined limits, but that is what parents do. However, there are fewer boundaries during the teen years, allowing his independence and leeway to make his own mistakes, while confirming how much you care for his wellbeing. When you put your trust in him, he is most likely to live up to your expectations.

There will be times when you want to discuss adult subjects with your teenager. When you have lively conversations about sex, drugs, alcohol, cigarettes, contraception, religion, politics and finances, his understanding of these many-sided topics will not be solely up to his school and his peers. Misinformation can be confusing, especially if it comes at him from questionable sources. Teens need to know the facts and dangers and, let's be honest, if you have been drinking or smoking for years, you cannot in good faith tell him not to drink or smoke. However, you can let him know the consequences and health dangers. He will decide for himself whether to follow your example or go his own way. There should be a give and take in these discussions, not simply you laying down the law. A teenager wants to be in charge of his destiny. It may even be easier for him to hear advice about sex, for example, from a favorite uncle, aunt, or grandparent than from his parents. Hearing family stories may bring up life lessons that will help him with his own decisions.

A good friend once asked me if I had given my teen the "talk." Here's Mike's version:

"One evening, I asked my teenage son if we could talk about something important," said Mike.

His son rolled his eyes and figured it was time for 'that talk,' or something embarrassing like that.

Mike replied, "It's not the sex talk. But, unfortunately, I have been diagnosed with an illness that lasts for about seven to ten years, if I'm lucky. My mind seems to have taken a vacation, and I might say things that are crazy, dumb, and just plain wrong. I'll do things that are embarrassing, and I won't even realize it. I will still be able to work, make money, buy food and pay for the roof over your head, but it won't be easy. I could really use your help to keep me straight and let me know when I'm messing up. When you are about twenty, my mind will begin to clear, and soon, I will be intelligent again, and I'll be able to say and do things that won't cause you to cringe. I am so grateful to have you around to help me out."[76]

It truly is amazing how the perception of a teen changes when he goes out on his own. When he looks back at his parents from the perspective of a self-supporting adult, he gains respect for how they managed to survive. Maybe they are not quite so lame after all, but individuals who have weathered storms and learned a few life lessons. Possibly, they handled things in an amazingly successful way, or maybe they made some life changing mistakes that they still struggle with. Parents then become mentors, embarrassingly confessing the mistakes they made, and happily talking about what things they did well. If the teen pays attention, he may be able to gain some insight on how to chart his own course.

Even though you are made to feel like you are bumbling your way through these teenage years, you are still the adult on the scene. Your kids are looking to you as their example, while critically watching your actions more than your words. Parents make adjustments too; hopefully with a good dose of humor, while remembering how things were when they were teens craving independence. The responsibility of making most of his choices and decisions is being transferred into your teen's hands.

When one of our daughters was in her mid-teens, we began to feel like we were becoming more authoritarian than we wanted to be. I thought I was my daughter's friend; now all of a sudden, I felt like the cops. "You came home too late. Where were you? Why didn't you tell us where you were going? You didn't do your chores. Your grades are slipping. You are getting sick from too little sleep." When my daughter and I had a talk, we came to an understanding that she was usually a responsible person, and not prone to getting into trouble, but as parents, we also had our concerns. One of the agreements that we decided on was to make a list of things that she could check off before going out on a date. Was her homework done and chores finished? Was she going out too often and not getting enough sleep? We trusted her judgment and after checking these things off of "the list," it was her decision whether it was the right time to go out with her friends. If she felt ready, she let us know her plans: Where she was going, who her date was, who would be driving, when they were leaving, and when we could expect her home. She learned personal responsibility from evaluating the situation and making smart plans. When mistakes were made, there was a chance for personal growth. She began to understand what was causing our anxiety and started to see things from our perspective. If she thought her schedule was sensible, it would probably be reasonable to us. Life settled down. It wasn't long before "the list" became passé, and good habits were established.

During her junior year of high school, she was the first member of the family to sign up to be an exchange student, spending a summer in The Dominican Republic. She later went to Costa Rica for a semester during college. Being on her own helped her grow into an independent individual able to make good choices, not to mention becoming fluent in Spanish. She is now a charge nurse in the ICU (Intensive Care Unit) of a San Francisco hospital, where her bilingual language skills are a big asset.

Finding those rare, unhurried occasions to spend time with your teenager reestablishes your connection. Playing games is a great way to have quality family time. *A game like Scruples was a fun way for us to bring up difficult adult situations. "Scruples" revolves around solving compromising dilemmas, such as cheating, sex, business fraud, stealing, and lying. Each card that was drawn brought up an interesting question, and we all had to guess how the person who was "it" would solve his problem. Inevitably, it created humorous and poignant discussions. Even today, the grandkids join the family in playing Monopoly, Life, Risk, Chess, Parcheesi, Jeopardy, and card games that bring up an ample dose of intriguing ideas about life, strategy, finances, competition, and sportsmanship. Bocce, golf, ultimate, Ping-Pong, hiking, basketball, and sailing are some of the outdoor sports that keep us active and our bodies fit.*

Long rides in the car, for example, give you an opportunity to share thoughts and ideas with your teenager. Religion, sex, finances, and politics are subjects that are especially interesting. Tales of your own experiences makes it more personal. Teenagers are trying to figure out for themselves the great mysteries of life. Resist the urge to pontificate about how you think it all should be, and let him express his ideas. If something seems to be bothering him, just being quiet might allow room for him to open up and talk about what he is feeling.

Teens love to talk about money. Let him know about your career, mortgage, investments, and taxes. Would he like to earn his own spending cash or save up for a car or something else that he really wants? With your assistance, he can open up his own bank account. An after school job is always good, as long as there is enough time for his studies and school activities. Introducing your teenager to the real world of work will give him a taste of the realities of life. "Take Your Child to Work Days" can be interesting when you are able to incorporate him into your schedule. Teens need to see how hard you work, what you do, and what it takes to support the family. After all, you are his role model in the real world. If your employer does not allow you to bring your child to work, perhaps you can find a relative or friend who can show him a part of the adult work world. Summer jobs and internships add to the work experience in the area that he finds most intriguing. This not only allows him to earn spending cash and handle his own expenses, but it may even present a possible connection and network for a future employment opportunity. Becoming an apprentice in a skill that he is interested in, with someone who can also be a wise mentor, may be one of the more valuable things a young teen can do to become acquainted with what life has to offer.

My tie-dye business, for example, became a good training ground for our kids and gave them a chance to work with us. They were well aware of where the food on the table came from and how the bills were paid. They might rather have slept in on Saturday mornings and done other things, but we rarely heard a complaint. Rising early, we would arrive at a craft fair before daylight to locate our booth and set up our display before the crowds arrived. The kids became great sales people: engaging with customers, helping them find what they were looking for, and closing the deal. Sometimes a nervous customer would want us to check on our nine-year-old daughter's math to make sure she had given the right price and the right change. It was almost always correct. Also, our accountant advised us to pay them well for their work. With their earnings, they bought their clothes, paid for their entertainment and saved for college. While they were learning life skills, we were able to spend many hours working alongside each other. There was laughter and good times while we sold our clothing throughout the long day. When it was time to tear down the booth and pack everything back into the van, everyone participated in a choreographed dance that brought the day to a pleasant close. In the playful competition of our family, we often timed the teardown to see if we could set a new record. Afterwards, over a tasty meal at a favorite restaurant, we would laugh about the highlights of the day's events. We downsized our business when our children began heading out on their own. Looking back on those years, we see that it was long hours of work, but the time we spent together was invaluable to our relationships. They all benefited from learning how to operate a small business, and some of our young adults went on to become successful entrepreneurs.

Giving your teen a chance to be independent and responsible will enhance his self-confidence. Every time he makes a choice about how to spend his own money, it makes him more financially savvy. Growing up with a college savings account lets him watch an investment grow towards a long-term goal.

Our son, Saul, bought a used Honda CRX with his own money and paid for the insurance. During his high school years, our eldest son, Brian, traveled across the country to attend The Farm reunions and visit family on the East Coast. He borrowed our van and paid for the trip out of his savings. When the other children became teenagers, they joined him on his road trips, each paying their share of gas and food, and experiencing adventures that were highlights of those years. The vehicle broke down in a small town, a highway patrolman pulled them over, relationships grew tense, and they learned to work out problems along the way.

Having a stake in their education and adventures puts fiscal responsibility onto your teen. Our children helped pay for their travels and college expenses. One of our sons paid for part of his education with work-study programs and loans. He told us that at three o'clock in the morning, with a big paper due, it was the fact that he was paying for it himself that gave him the impetus to finish the assignment.

Encouraging our children to step out of not only the town where they lived, but also, the U.S.A., opened their eyes to the wide world around them while taking them to another level of independence. In high school, Audrey, Rose, Caitlin, and Olivia each spent a year in a Spanish-speaking country living with a family as exchange students with the American Field Service (AFS), a Quaker organization. The AFS student exchange program was formed after World War II, having operated ambulances (they were pacifists) during both world wars. Their idea was to offer intercultural learning opportunities to help students develop the knowledge, skills, and understanding needed to create a more just and peaceful world. Today, there have been more than 424,000 young people who have gone abroad to 99 countries.[77]

During their college years, our daughters also took part in the exchange programs offered by the University of California. They became fluent in another language, gained respect for a different culture, and acquired a planetary consciousness. Amazingly, the cost was nearly the same whether they stayed home or went abroad.

Life often brings it's own lessons to our worldly classroom. Before she left to Venezuela, Rose was in a minor car accident. When the police officer came to make a report, he said, "It's not *if* teenage drivers get into an accident, it's **when**." In effect, he had made a profound statement about teens in general, that they are learning about becoming an adult at the same time they are learning to drive. There will be misjudgments and accidents. Fortunately, it was only a fender-bender, but it shook Rose up and gave her an expanded awareness of her *responsibility as a driver.*

Teens will have these kinds of growing up events. If it is not the car, you can be sure it will be something. Being on good terms with your teenager means that you will be there to help them when they have a problem. When you focus on the positive, disciplining and correcting become passé and adult-to-adult conversations become the norm. If you treat her with respect when there are mistakes, she will learn and move on, wiser than before. Experimenting is what teenagers do and, hopefully, you can be their guide when they need you.

While a teen is exploring her world, the responsibilities at home prepare her for the inevitable everyday chores of life. Keeping the house in working order requires everyone's help. *We had a chore chart of things that needed to be done each day and, often late in the afternoon when everyone was home, we would call a "Blitz Time" where each person joined in to clean up. Each kid would call out their job and go do it. Within a half hour or so, it was all done and the house would be back in decent shape. When we did this once a day, our house was clean and neat, at least for a while.*

Then there was the inevitable day when each of our children walked across the high school stage to receive their diploma. It was such a proud moment that it was hard not to tear up when Pomp and Circumstance cascaded through the air, heralding this big step. Watching them take off to college and the uncharted frontier of their lives was the next chapter in their great adventure.

This transition after high school usually includes awesome parties, summer jobs, and then off to college, or to the world of work. A few seniors have even saved up enough to travel to Europe or Asia. They inevitably find out more about who they are and in what direction they really want to go.

At this point in many cultures around the world, there is some kind of initiation ceremony for a young adult to begin an active role in the community. In some tribal traditions, the father and other men of the clan would ceremoniously separate the teenage boy from his mother. He was required to go through tests of endurance, skill, and strength, as well as a quest for the spiritual meaning to his life. A girl, honored in her passage to womanhood, was tutored and counseled by her mother and the women of the clan about birthing and raising children, family, food gathering, medicinal herbs, as well as tanning, weaving, and food preparation for the winter, etc. After these ceremonies, there was no question that these young people were about to take their place as adults in their community, ready to marry, become parents, and help insure the wellbeing of the tribe.

Unfortunately, in our society we hardly stop to evaluate, contemplate, and have a ceremony for these milestones. Our culture could benefit from an updated version of The Rite of Passage.

The Rite of Passage

Passing a driver's test and receiving a license is about as close to a rite of passage as a young adult gets these days. In California, for instance, when you are issued a license, you are automatically registered to vote, a privilege that allows you to put a mark on the political process. Walking the stage to receive a high school or college diploma is an acknowledgment of an achievement and celebrates future aspirations. However, these rites do not specifically call for the young adult to join his community as a full-fledged member.

There are various ceremonies within the religious communities like bar mitzvahs, confirmations, and quinceaneras, but these are generally for young people from 12 to 15. In our modern society, where attending school pushes back the age when teens leave home, there is little opportunity for our 16-22 year olds to be embraced by their community into the shared responsibilities of adulthood. During this time of their lives, wise mentors can be beneficial. It could be a valuable addition, if we offered a relevant ceremony and celebration that welcomed these young adults into the grown-up world. It could facilitate a balance between the coming out of the young adult into his or her maturity and keeping family bonds intact.

Two interesting books that discuss rites of passage are Barry Spector's *Madness at the Gates of the City* and Angus Ramsey's *Sally's Gift*.[78]

If anyone is interested in working to create such a ceremony, you can start such a rite among your family and community of friends. There are also groups that have started this process and would welcome participation.[79]

The Roaring Twenties

The transition into adulthood that begins in the teen years often culminates when the young adult graduates from high school or college. Although a parent's job is never done, you can now take a step back and allow your baby bird to fly the nest. Developing a new adult-to-adult relationship is usually a challenging exercise for all concerned, especially when your grown child stumbles and makes mistakes. As a parent, you are no longer in charge. Even when you ask politely if she would like to hear your opinion, be prepared for her to not be interested in hearing your advice. Your fledgling adult wants to succeed on her own terms. She will follow her own counsel and trail markers, busy with her own life, job, and friends.

There will be wonderful times when your young adult visits and spends vacation time with you. She will probably chow down on her favorite foods and feel the comfort of family like in the old days. Talking about what and how she is doing opens up friendly discussions, and they may even ask for advice on such things as buying a car, finding the right job, or looking for a place to live. Telling your stories of how it was when you were young and first starting out on your own, dating, getting a job, the mistakes you made, might be interesting to her. Then, before you know it, she might want to introduce you to her new love.

Through the normal trials and errors, adult children usually figure out how to take care of themselves. When our "20 something" kids asked for financial help with a loan or co-signing a student financial package for graduate school, we treated them like adults. Whatever it is, making up a formal agreement about the transaction, the interest rate, and a reasonable payment schedule is advisable. Paying back a loan usually breaks the financial dependency between parent and child and is a valuable lesson in personal responsibility and financial realities.

Did she move back home for a while to save up for school, or during a difficult transition in her life? Are you going to ask her to pay rent, and contribute to the financial and domestic responsibilities of the household? Having your child carry her own weight may be one of the most difficult things that you have ever required, but it would be a disservice to her otherwise. She will probably appreciate the lesson later on, and you will not fall into a co-dependency of continuing the parent/child relationship.

Young people in their 20's are generally waiting longer to be married, and are having children later in life, if they choose that path at all. Before long they might traverse the bridge into marriage and children.

If and when grandchildren come, it's often a time when you are asked to help out. The new parents might actually be interested in your advice on child rearing and will enjoy hearing your stories of how it was raising them. There are new parents who want to do it their own way and, when that happens, you can take a back seat helping them out when you are asked. It's one of the highlights of life to be in the presence of grandchildren. You feel years younger, keeping up with their boundless energy. The love that flows is something special, and grandchildren who have close bonds with their grandparents blossom with the added attention.

A Return to the Big World

After living our Utopian dream for twelve years in Tennessee and satellite farms in Wisconsin, Alabama, and Florida, Robert and I decided to move our large family back to California. The Farm had been going through a time of upheaval after having realized that the communal financial plan was not viable. It was time to change to a cooperative economy where each family supported themselves and also paid into a fund to maintain community services. The communal dream was over, and we had learned certain lessons that would prove to be valuable for our next stage of life. We had loved living on The Farm, but it was one thing to bet our lives on the "noble experiment" and it was another to risk our children's future. We also felt it was important for our kids to have the opportunity to attend the University of California system. In 1983 we settled in Modesto, a town in the Central Valley, east of San Francisco, which had affordable housing for our large brood.

When we left the community, there was no golden handshake or pension. So, Robert worked off The Farm with friends at a construction site for several months to finance the big move. Both of our families were kind enough to also chip in some travel money. An old station wagon that we bought for $200 was fixed up in the motor pool for our cross-country trek and off we went.

When we arrived in California, we spent a few weeks living at campsites in our car and small tents while we searched for a rental that we could afford. After paying for the first and last month's rent, and a deposit for a four-bedroom home with a pool, we had $50 to our name. $10 was spent on watermelon and vegetables at the local produce stand to go with the beans and flour that we had brought with us from Tennessee. My multi-talented husband had already found work and the last of our cash was reserved for his gas money. The kids thought they were in Paradise, with a nice house, a fruit salad, and a pool to call their own.

Robert immediately went to work plying one of his many trades - roofing for a local contractor. He could always get a job as a roofer, even though at the time unemployment was at an all time high in the Central Valley. With a portion of his first paychecks, I bought an old washing machine and a couple of dozen T-shirts and dye. Once again, I started my tie-dyed art-wear business, with its humble beginnings in our garage (what else is a young hippie with a bunch of kids to do?). Our children were soon settled into the nearby public schools for the first time, and it wasn't long before we were firmly entrenched in the suburban world.

In a few short years, with a loan from my parents, we were able to put a down payment on a home. Our businesses quickly outgrew the garage, and when the dismal housing market recovered, we were able to refinance our home and buy a commercial property that was a fixer-upper. Robert's remodeling skills came in handy, and our businesses took off, catching a wave of prosperity. The downtown craftsman house was large enough to include our new musical instrument business and we named our company Harmony Enterprises, a name that would include all of our endeavors.

We were able to use the skills we had developed on The Farm, from roofing to carpentry, from making tie-dyes to running a business. But, even then, as with anyone just starting out in a new business, home, and location, there was a transition period. Understanding how inter-personal relationships worked with neighbors, customers, and fellow business people helped make things flow smoothly. Having built up our toolbox of communication, we were able to weather storms, work out kinks, make bold moves to start businesses, and jump into the workplace wherever we could.

Taking things a step at a time, doing what needed to be done in the present moment was our yoga. Having a vision and a purpose to see our children thrive, finish college and follow their dreams into adulthood kept us on our daily track.

Of course, we had what we called the usual "somethings." These were the car or washing machine breakdowns, the reject letter from a show promoter, a customer who wouldn't pay, etc. Sometimes there would be a respite and then two or three upsets would come at once. Taking them in stride was another yoga. It was a thrill to watch our dreams become realities and our sweat equity pay off. Watching our children cross the stages in high school and college was a time to celebrate, honoring their hard work and success. They were on the next step of life's adventure.

The Empty Nest

Cutting the apron strings and returning home to an empty nest is a time for you to celebrate the liberation out of the daily routines and responsibilities of parenthood. The boundless, creative energy that you needed for raising your child since his conception can now be redirected to new avenues of expression. Discovering your own hidden passions, that you have ignored while you were a parent, can be placed front and center. This is a time to re-direct your energies and re-imagine this next stage of life.[80]

It's as relevant for you to pursue your next step, as it is to let your young adult leave home and find his place in the world. You look at your partner across the table while clinking wine glasses and then wonder why you are still at home. Without the schedules and obligations of child rearing, you are free to spread your own wings and soar. There are dynamic and unique outlets for this newly released creativity. It's like a second honeymoon and it can be spontaneous to make love, in any room of the house at any time of the day or night. A new you can subtlety emerge, not the Mom or Dad that you have been for so many years. There are adjustments to make while becoming accustomed to the transition. Once this changeover is embraced, you will be on your way to fulfilling your dreams.

We paid college tuition to the Board of Regents of the University of California for sixteen years. When our last daughter, Olivia, left Modesto for the University of California, Santa Barbara, Robert and I went cruising aboard our sailboat, Harmony. Since 2000, we have been sailing in Mexico for six months of each year with an extended three-year trip through Central America to Ecuador and back to Mexico between 2006-2008. You can read more about our adventures in **"Harmony on the High Seas, When Your Mate Becomes Your Matey,"**[81]

In the fall of 2003, Brian, our eldest son, purchased Harmony Enterprises and with his wife, Heather, and son, Onyx, is successfully carrying on the family business. Our children, and now grandchildren, take time off from their busy lives to visit us during the holidays aboard Harmony, and we return each summer to spend time with the family and work on our houses.

Before we knew it, we had six grandchildren, five within five years. We helped the new families almost every day for a month after each baby was born, keeping the household running while Mom and Dad were able to bond with their newborn. When the grandchildren were from six to ten years old and were content with spending nights away from their parents, we held Nana/Baba Camp. Each summer, the parents would have a week-long break while the cousins spent wonderful times together swimming, doing crafts and playing games. There would be field trips to the local Planetarium and Natural History Museum. Each child gave us a few countries that they wanted to visit, and we'd watch movies from the library about Australia, India, Italy, New Zealand, and the Galapagos. Last year we took the camp on the road, spending a week exploring Crater Lake in Oregon and a fabulous weekend watching the totality of the solar eclipse. The time the kids spend together is filled with laughter and fun and deepens the family connections.

Having a love that lasts has been our focus throughout our marriage and continues to be our lifework. Living on our sailboat, Harmony, for half of each year has allowed us to have amazing adventures, visit exotic places, and meet fascinating people from many cultures. As a special bonus, it has given us endless time and space to enjoy each other surrounded by nature's beauty.

May love be with you always on your challenging, rewarding adventures.

Part 3: Taking the Test

Below you will find a copy of the 101 Question Compatibility Test found in Book 1. These are questions, which are ideally taken as a pre-marital test. The results will point out areas where you are compatible and a few places where there will be differences. When you use it as a starting point for discussions and compromises it can bring you closer together. Nobody fails this test; everyone passes!

To answer the questions, find a comfortable and quiet place away from your partner where you won't be rushed or distracted. Try to resist the temptation to give answers that will please your love. Be true to yourself.

Later, in a relaxed setting, compare and discuss your answers. The subjects where you see eye to eye confirm your compatibility. Celebrate! The answers that you disagree about are the issues that will need work. You'll find the answers to the questions in Book 1, *How to Find Love and Make It Last.* Refer to them if you're interested in delving further into specifics. Can your differences be reconciled? Can you change your ways that make you difficult to live with? There's no better time than now to discuss these issues and reach a clear understanding.

Answer the questions with Agree, Disagree, Unsure, Yes, No, or Maybe. Be prepared to talk about why you chose those answers. While you go through the test, place a star by any question that makes you uncomfortable, or brings up a subject that you have never considered before.

The 101 Question Compatibility Test

Mark each question with: Agree, Disagree, Unsure, Yes, No or Maybe

1. Do you enjoy your work?

2. Will you make a good parent?

3. Are your in-laws comfortable with your culture or religion?

4. Does your partner's sense of humor sometimes bother you?

5. Do you enjoy spending time with your partner's friends?

6. Do you have any doubts that you have made the right choice?

7. Are you concerned that there is a significant age difference between you?

8. Have you grown up with a healthy attitude about sex?

9. Do you agree on your roles of caretaker and/or breadwinner when rearing your children?

10. Do either of you have large debts?

11. Do you know where you are going to live?

12. Have issues concerning premarital sex, former lovers, and/or spouses caused problems?

13. Does your partner become angry, making you afraid that s/he will hurt you?

14. a.) Are you worried about you or your partner's use of tobacco, alcohol, or other addictive substances?

    b.) Do one or both of you enjoy drinking or using recreational drugs in moderation?

15. Do you have an agreement about how to handle your finances?

16. Are there conflicts concerning your religious beliefs?

17. Is your partner frequently moody or depressed?

18. When there are problems to be discussed, does your partner refuse to talk about them?

19. Are you uncomfortable with your partner's public show of affection?

20. Do you enjoy discussions about religion, philosophy and spiritual matters?

21. Did you take an active part in the wedding plans?

22. Is one or both of you a workaholic?

23. Do you agree about whether or not to have children?

24. Do you work out your problems by having sex?

25. Does your partner make condescending remarks to or about you?

26. Are there family members who will cause friction in your relationship?

27. Will your partner make a good parent?

28. Does your partner encourage you in your interests? (Your career, hobbies, sports, art, music, yoga, etc.)

29. Have you talked about how you want to maintain your home and do your household chores? (Doing the dishes, laundry, the lawn, vacuuming, cleaning the bathrooms, etc.)

30. Does your partner have certain habits that annoy you? (List them.)

31. Are you uncomfortable when you are with the in-laws?

32. Do you feel pressure to choose a certain spiritual or religious path?

33. Is you partner jealous and possessive of you?

34. Is your partner or you not on speaking terms with a member(s) of your family?

35. Does your partner refuse to compromise on a particular issue? (List it.)

36. Do you believe in the power of love to heal the body, mind, and spirit?

37. Do you have 'my' and 'your' friends, but only a few who you share in common?

38. Do you believe that sex is an important part of

marriage, and are you open to exploring the art of lovemaking with your partner?

39. Did your partner want to get married sooner than you did?

40. Do you agree about how you are going to discipline your children?

41. Are you confident that your income will cover your expenses; can you live within your budget?

42. Does financial help from your family have strings attached?

43. Do you both have promising careers?

44. Do you and your partner handle your personal problems in a reasonable way?

45. Does your partner's behavior at social events sometimes embarrass you?

46. Do one or both of you always have to be right?

47. Do you or your partner have a tendency to be lazy or unmotivated?

48. Do you agree on how to furnish and decorate your home?

49. Do you know what is sexually satisfying for your partner?

50. Do you agree on how much of your budget will be spent on housing?

51. Are there homosexual, bisexual, or trans-sexual tendencies and preferences in your relationship?

52. Is it difficult to talk about your true feelings with your partner?

53. Were you feeling pressured into marriage by the family?

54. Do you worry that problems you experienced in childhood will affect the way you raise your children?

55. Are you nervous and uncomfortable about revealing your body to your partner?

56. Can you count on your partner to be a good listener?

57. Are you worried that you do not have adequate insurance coverage?

58. Do you and your partner trust each other with members of the opposite sex?

59. Are you unhappy with one or more of your partner's interests (career, hobbies, sports, etc.)?

60. Are you sometimes embarrassed by your partner's appearance?

61. Did you disagree about the type of wedding you wanted? Did it turn out okay?

62. Do you try to avoid arguments or disagreements with your partner?

63. Does your partner handle his/her finances responsibly?

64. What are your expectations for your children?

65. Do you have doubts about your love for your partner?

66. Are you uncomfortable with your partner's family and friends since you have come from a different social, cultural, or economic background?

67. Can you count on your partner to give you support when you are feeling down?

68. Is your partner too dependent on his or her parents?

69. Are you ready to accept the responsibilities of being a parent, (3 A.M. feedings, a sick and crying child, "terrible twos," rebellious teens)?

70. Is there a difference between love and sex?

71. Are you comfortable with your partner's politics?

72. Are TV and video games a satisfying and inexpensive pastime for you?

73. When you are angry, do you say or do hurtful things to your partner?

74. Will your different educational backgrounds cause problems?

75. Have you talked about using birth control to plan your family?

76. Are you satisfied and happy with how your life is going?

77. Are you afraid that you might be sexually impotent or frigid?

78. Are your ideas about raising children compatible?

79. Are there problems resulting from an interracial marriage?

80. Is there a conflict about your views on adoption?

81. Is your partner involved in community activities at the expense of you and the family?

82. Does your partner support your future goals and ambitions?

83. Are your partner's eating habits a source of contention?

84. Can you talk with each other about any subject?

85. Do your partner's prejudices bother you?

86. Did getting married solve some of your problems?

87. When you have time off, does your partner choose all of the activities?

88. Do you agree that both of you will be working outside of the home?

89. Do you embrace the basic principles of the traditional marriage vows?

90. Are you and your partner on the same sleep cycles?

91. Will the physical and/or mental health of one or both of you cause any problems?

92. Does your partner place too much emphasis on neatness?

93. Do you have trouble agreeing on major expenditures (House, car, vacation)?

94. In the middle of a heated argument, can you agree to a cooling-off period before you try to resolve the issue?

95. Are you living too close to the parents?

96. Were you mentally, physically, emotionally or sexually abused as a child?

97. Did pregnancy affect your marriage plans?

98. Have you had sex before this relationship?

99. Are you in agreement about how you like to spend your vacation and holiday times?

100. Have you talked about how you want your life to be?

101. Do you feel relaxed and comfortable with your partner?

How did The Test Go for You?

Do you share similar views on the big questions like children, finances, and your visions for the future? Did you talk about your conflicting answers and any issues that they brought up? Can you sort through disagreements and come out the other side still loving each other? Are you learning how to operate your relationship respectfully? Are your communication skills improving?

You might like to review the chapters on The Subconscious and Communication for more guidelines to help discussions remain kind, helpful, and compassionate, instead of escalating into frustrated shouting matches.

Can you talk about everything? Have you both had to make some changes? Has it been done for the good of you individually and for the health of your relationship? There's no doubt that when your partner shares her concerns, it sometimes feels as if she is smashing your whole world. If you decide to forgo this process of working it out, inevitably you will continue to come up against the same issues. To a new couple, this can be alarming, and you may want to give up or run away. Fortunately, with practice, you can learn how to let go of deeply rooted habits and negative belief systems, and evolve towards having a greater capacity for love and happiness.

Acknowledgments

I want to thank Ina May Gaskin and the late Stephen Gaskin, and everyone on the intentional spiritual community known as The Farm, who were profound influences in my life and the lives of my family. I particularly want to thank you for all of those late nights when you truly lived the practice of helping us sort out the intricate workings of our psyches. There were times when your words made the difference, when you taught me the meaning of unconditional love, and you empowered me when you once told me to "tie myself to the mast during the storm and hold on."

My gratitude is also boundless for The Farm midwives who delivered our children into a world filled with love and support while being surrounded by the beauty of nature.

Special thanks goes to Deanna Roozendaal, an English professor and fellow sailor, who edited my manuscript, giving positive and supportive feedback. My sincere appreciation goes to Margaret Murray, Marion Van Der Pol, and Jan Hudson who were also my editors and helped bring this book into reality. Irene Song, my talented and helpful daughter-in-law has given of her time and expertise to help create the covers of Book 1 and Book 2, and generously gave many hours of technical instruction and valuable feedback. Sally Gerbo of Gerbo Designs was my creative graphic designer. Thank you all for your interest in birthing this book.

My deepest appreciation goes out to our son, Saul and daughter, Olivia Gleser, who gave of their busy schedules to provide insights from their youthful perspectives. Our wonderful children have given me their love and support. Celebration also goes out to our grandchildren, who bring us joy, sweeten our lives with their kindness, beauty, humor, and intelligence, and ensure bright prospects for the future.

> **Appreciation, Gratitude, and Celebration!**
>
> **Thank you all!**

Appendix A:

Reading References by Subject

Loving Yourself

In the book, *Core Transformation, Reaching the Wellspring Within* by Connirae and Tamara Andreas,[82] there is the Core State Exercise that describes how to reach deep into your psyche to heal your body, mind, and spirit. Also, they give exercises on how to parent the child of your youth.

Carolyn Myss's book, *Why People Don't Heal and How They Can* says, "Regardless of what needs surface as you learn to know and love yourself, the important points are to give yourself the **right of choice, self-expression, and self-respect**."[83]

The complex subject of change has attracted many great authors over the years like Jon Kabat-Zinn who wrote the great book, *Wherever You Go, There You Are.*[84]

What the Bleep Do We Know written by William Arntz, Betsy Chasse, and Mark Vicente,[85] is a fascinating book that was also turned into a great movie.

Byron Katie's book, *Loving What Is,*[86] describes a simple and helpful method of getting to the bottom of any problem and finding healing and true freedom.

You might like taking the *"Passion Test,"* (2008) by Chris and Janet Attwood[87] or read inspiring books that encourage you to take a step to follow your dream such as *The Secret (2006)* and *The Power, (The Secret)* (2010) by Rhonda Byrne,[88] and *The Divine Matrix* by Gregg Braden (2007).[89] Also books by Deepak Chopra, Wayne Dyer, and Eckart Tolle give you illuminating and motivational ways to find that healing place within.[90] The inspirational author of many books, Louise Hay,[91] writes, "Life is very simple. We create our experiences by our thinking and feeling patterns. What we believe about ourselves and about life becomes true for us." Mike Dooley, in his daily inspirations at the universe@tut.com says that "Thoughts Become Things."

A great group of fun exercises to tap into how to make changes for yourself are found in Sharon Franquemont's book, *You Already Know What To Do.*[92]

Terrence Real wrote the wonderful book about dealing with depression called *I Don't Want to Talk About It.*[93]

Relationships

Lew and Francine Epstein, and Reppy Epstein Kirkilis' book *Trusting You Are Loved*[94] is filled with a deep-seated and heart filled look at love. When we trust that we are loved, life takes on a whole new positive outlook and begins the journey of making a relationship work well. Beautiful emphasis is placed on compassion, listening, apology, forgiveness, speaking from the heart, and commitment, all seemingly simple concepts, but as Lew says, "It's simple, but not easy."

Harville Hendrix, in his books, *Keeping the Love You Find,* and *Getting the Love You Want,*[95] has you delving deep into the origins of relationship problems with excellent tools to bring love into your life.

Byron Katie's book, *Loving What Is*,[96] and *I Need Your Love, Is that True*, describes a simple and helpful method of getting to the bottom of any problem and finding healing and true freedom.

If your partner has cheated on you, try "*Not 'Just Friends': "Rebuilding Trust and Recovering Your Sanity After Infidelity*," by Shirley P. Glass with Jean Coppock Staehili (2004, Atria Books.)[97]

Two books about the continuum of sexual preferences are John Money's *Gay, Straight, and In-Between: The Sexology of Sexual Orientation*, and Simon LeVay's *The Sexual Brain*.[98]

Joel Crohn, Ph.D. wrote a helpful book entitled *Mixed Match, How to Create Successful Interracial, Interethnic, and Interfaith Relationships*.[99]

Your Body, Health and Sexuality

An excellent source of information for women is Dr. Christine Northrup's books like *Women's Body, Women's Wisdom*.[100]

Jed Diamond has also written a number of books with information about men's cycles including *The Irritable Male Syndrome: Managing the Four Key Causes of Depression and Aggression*.[101]

A book that can give you a look at a wide range of women's sexual experiences is *Shared Intimacies, Women's Sexual Experiences* by Lonnie Barbach, PH.D and Linda Levine, A.C.S.W.[102]

If you are wondering about testing for sexually transmitted diseases you might go to the National HIV &

STD Testing at https://gettested.cdc.gov, and Anonymous testing at www.planned parenthood.org/learn/stds/std-testing-hiv-safer-sex/hiv-aids/hiv-testing and free STD testing at www.freestdcheck.org.[103]

Handling Your Anger

The Dance of Anger by Harriet Goldhor Lerner Ph.D.[104]

Gary Chapman and Ross Campbell in their book, *The Five Love Languages of Children* and Gary Chapman in his book, *The Other Side of Love,* are resources on understanding rage, and how to distinguish between valid and distorted anger.[105]

Harville Hendrix, in his book, *Getting the Love You Want,*[106] has you delving deep into the origins of relationship problems with excellent tools to bring love into your life.

Raising Children

New enlightened ways of working it out with your kids are discussed in *How to Talk to Kids So They Will Listen, and How to Listen to Kids So They Will Talk*, by Faber and Mazlish (Revised 1999), and *The Five Love Languages for Children,* by Chapman and Campbell (2012).[107]

Dr. Kevin Leman's books, *The Birth Order Book, Why You are the Way You Are* and *Keeping Your Family Together While the World is Falling Apart*[108] among others, are enlightening and helpful when understanding yourself in relation to your family and with raising children.

If there is an unfortunate break or problem with a teen or adult child, Joshua Coleman, Ph.D. has written *When Parents Hurt, Compassionate Strategies When You and Your Grown Child Don't Get Along.*[109] Dr. Fred Luskin's *Forgive for Good, A Proven Prescription for Health and Happiness*[110] is also very helpful for problems with adult children and life's difficulties in general.

Financial Advice

Suze Ormond's,[111] *The Nine Steps to Financial Freedom*, and Dave Ramsey's book. *The Total Money Makeover*[112] are both easy to read with a no-nonsense, balanced attitude about financial matters.

Abusive Childhood

Adult Survivors of Child Abuse at www.naasca.org/010111-Recovery.htm, www.psychecentral.com, www.Isurvive.org, www.adultchildren.org, and Rape, Abuse and Incest national Network at http:/www/rainn.org/adult-survivors-of-childhood-sexual-abuse.[113]

Byron Katie's, *Loving What Is* also is a valuable resource.[114]

Problems and Estrangement with Teens and Adult Children

Two excellent books on handling difficult situations with teens and adult children are Dr. Joshua Coleman's *When Parents Hurt, Compassionate Strategies When You and Your Grown Child don't Get Along*[115] and Dr. Fred Luskin's *Forgive for Good, A Proven Prescription for Health and Happiness.*[116]

Bibliography

Ackroyd, Eric. *A Dictionary of Dream Symbols.* London, UK: Blandford, 1993.

Andreas, Connirae and Tamara. *Core Transformation, Reaching the Wellspring Within.* Moab, Utah: Real People Press, 1994.

Arntz, William; Chasse, Betsy; Vicente, Mark. *What the Bleep Do We Know.* Deerfield Beach, FL: Health Communications, Inc., 2007.

Attwood, Janet and Chris. *The Passion Test, The Effortless Path to Discovering Your Life Purpose.* New York, NY: Penguin Group, 2006.

Barbach, Lonnie and Levine, Linda. *Shared Intimacies, Women's Sexual Experiences.* New York, NY: Bantam Books, 1989.

Bradshaw, John. *Homecoming.* New York, NY: Bantam Books, 1990.

Bradshaw, John. John Bradshaw on: *Healing the Shame that Binds You.* Deerfield Beach, FL: Health Connections, Inc., 1988.

Braden, Gregg. *The Divine Matrix.* Carlsbad, CA.: Hay House. Inc., 2007.

Byrne, Rhonda. *The Secret.* New York, NY: Simon and Schuster, Inc., 2006.

Byrne, Rhonda. New York, NY: Simon and Schuster, Inc., 2010

Chapman, Gary. *The Five Love Languages: The Secret to Love that Lasts.* Chicago, IL: Northfield Publishing, 2015.

Chapman, Gary and Campbell, Ross. *The Five Love Languages of Children.* Chicago, IL: Northfield Publishing, 2012.

Chapman, Gary. *The Other Side of Love.* Chicago, IL: Moody Press, 1999.

Chopra, Deepak. *Creating Affluence, The A-to-Z Steps to*

a Richer Life. San Rafael, CA: Amber-Allen Publishing, 1998.
Coelho, Paulo and Clarke, Alan R. *The Alchemist*. New York, NY: Harper Collins Publisher, 1998.
Coelho, Paulo. *By the River Peidra I Sat Down and Wept*. New York, NY: Harper Collins Publishers, Inc., 1997.
Coleman, Joshua, Ph.D. *When Parents Hurt, Compassionate Strategies When You and Your Grown Child Don't Get Along*. New York, NY: Harper Collins Publishers, Inc., 2008.
Darling, Lynn. *For Better and Worse*. Esquire. May 1996, pg., 58-66
Deangelis, Barbara. M.D. *Secrets About Men Every Woman Should Know*. New York, NY: Dell Publishing, 1990.
Della-Madre, Leslene. *Midwifing Death, Returning to the Arms of the Ancient Mother*. Austin, TX: Plain View Press, 2003
Dooley, Mike. *Choose them Wisely: Thought Become Things*. New York, NY: Simon and Schuster. www.tut.com 2009.
Dooley, Mike. *The Top Ten Things Dead People Want to Tell You*. www.hayhouse.com, Hay House. 2014.
Dyer, Wayne W. *There's a Spiritual Solution to Every Problem*. New York, Harper Collins Publishers, 2001
Edelman, Hope. *Motherless Daughters, the Legacy of Loss*. New York, NY: Dell Publishing, 1994.
Epstein, Lew, Epstein, Francine, Kirkilis, Rebby Epstien. *Trusting Your Are Loved*. The Partnership Foundation, 1998, 2014.
Faber, Adele and Mazlish, Elaine. *How to Talk to Kids So Kids Will Listen and Listen So Kids Will Talk*. New York, NY: Avon Books, Inc., 1980, Revised. 1999.
Franquemont, Sharon. *You Already Know What To Do*, New York, NY: Penguin Putnam, Inc., 1999.
Gaskin, Ina May. *Ina May's Guide to Childbirth*. New York, NY: Bantam Dell, 2002.
Gaskin, Ina May. *Spiritual Midwifery*. Summertown, TN:

The Book Publishing Company, 1977.
Gaskin, Stephen. *This Season's People*. Summertown, TN: The Book Publishing Company, 1975.
Gleser, Virginia. *Harmony on the High Seas, When Your Mate Become Your Matey*, Modesto, CA: Harmony Publishing, 2011.
Gleser, Virginia. *How to Find Love and Make It Last, A Practical Guide to Relationships, Includes the 101 Question Compatibility Test, Book 1,* Modesto, CA: Harmony Publishing, 2016.
Gottman, John, Ph.D. *Why Marriages Succeed or Fail and How you Can Make Yours Last.* New York, NY: Fireside, Simon and Schuster, Inc., 1994.
Grey, John. *Men are From Mars, Women are from Venus: The Classic Guide to Understanding the Opposite Sex.* New York, NY: Harper Collins Publishers, Inc., 2012.
Gurian, Michael. *The Wonder of Boys.* New York, NY: Penguin Putman, Inc., 1996.
Gurian, Michael. *The Wonder of Girls.* Atria Books, New York, NY: Simon and Schuster, 2002.
Hafen, Bruce. *Marriage and the State's Legal Posture Toward the Family.* Vital speeches of the Day. Oct. 15, 1995, pg., 17-19
Harley, Willard F., Jr. *His Needs, Her Needs, Building an Affair Proof Marriage.* Grand Rapids, MI: Revell Publishing. 2011
Hay, Louise L. *Heal Your Body.* Carlsbad, Ca.: Hay House, Inc., 1982.
Hay, Louise L. *The Power is Within You.* Carson, Ca.: Hay House, Inc., 1991.
Hendrix, Harville. Ph.D. *Getting the Love You Want.* New York, NY: Henry Holt Company LLC., 1988.
Hendrix, Harville. Ph.D. *Keeping the Love You Find.* New York, NY: Atria Books, 1992.
Jeffers, Susan, Ph.D. *Feel the Fear and Do It Anyway.* New York, NY: Fawcett Columbine, 1987.

Katie, Byron and Mitchell, Stephen. *Loving What Is: Four Questions That Can Change Your Life.* New York, NY: Three Rivers Press, 2002.
Katie, Byron, with Michael Katz. *I Need Your Love – Is That True?* New York, NY: Three Rivers Press, 2005.
Kornfield, Jack. *After the Ecstasy, the Laundry, How the Heart Grows Wise on the Spiritual Path.* New York, NY: Bantam Books, 2000.
Lawler, Michael. *Doing Marriage Preparation Right.* America. Dec. 30, 1995-Jan 6, 1996, pg., 12-14
Leman, Dr. Kevin. *Keeping Your Family Together When the World is Falling Apart.* New York, NY: Delacorte Press, 1992
Leman, Dr. Kevin. *The Birth Order Book, Why You Are the Way You Are.* Grand Rapids, MI: Revell Publishing, 2009
Lerner, Harriet Goldhor. Ph.D. *The Dance of Anger.* New York, NY: Harper and Row Publishers, 1985.
Luskin, Dr. Fred, *Forgive for Good, A Proven Prescription for Health and Happiness.* New York, NY: Harper Collins Publishers, Inc., 2002.
The Miami Herald. May 19, 1980. Archives.
Miller, Matthew. *The Sacred "M."* The New Yorker. Oct. 1995, pg., 9-10
Millman, Dan. *Way of the Peaceful Warrior, A Book That Changes Lives.* Tiburon, CA: H. J. Kramer, Inc., 1984
Moore, Robert and Gillette, Douglas. *King, Warrior, Magician, Lover.* New York, NY: Harper Collins Publishers, 1990.
Myss, Caroline, PH.D. *Why People Don't Heal and How They Can.* New York, NY: Three River Press, 1997.
The New York Times Magazine. Oct. 8, 1995, pg., 51-63, 74-106
Northrup, Christine, M.D. *The Wisdom of Menopause.* New York, NY: Bantam Books, 2001.
Northrup, Christine, M.D. *Women's Bodies, Women's Wisdom.* New York, NY: Bantam Books, 1994.

Endnotes

1 www.cdc.gov, Center for Disease Control and Prevention and Huffingtonpost.com. In 2009 in a Huffington Post article 46% of more recently married couples failed to reach their 25th anniversary. A young couple marrying for the first time today has a lifetime divorce rate of 40%. 8.8 years is the average length of a marriage in the U.S. States vary on divorce rates.
2 www.guttmacher.org, Pregnancy statistics. In 2011 55% of pregnancies were mistimed (27%) or were unwanted (18%) out of 6.1 million pregnancies in the US.
3 www.aauw.org/research/the-simple-truth-about-the-gender-pay-gap 22% average pay gap between men and women in nearly every occupation both female-dominated, gender-balance and male-dominated workplaces. 9% pay gap in Washington, DC to 34% gap in Louisiana.
4 Adapted from a quote by the Roman philosopher, Seneca the Younger (4 BC-AD 65) who was quoting his friend Demetrius the Cynic. En-wikiquote.org/wiki/Seneca_the_Younger. Gregory K. Ericksen attributed the quote to Seneca in his book, *Women Entrepreneurs Only: 12 Women Entrepreneurs Tell the Stories of Their Success*.pg. ix. (1999)
5 Wilcox, Bradford. The Evolution of Divorce. National Affairs, Issue # 1, Fall 2009. From 1960-1980 the yearly divorce rate doubled from 9.2 per 1000 to 22.6 per 1000 marriages. In 2007 there were 17.5 per 1000 divorces so it is improving. 20% of couples married in 1950 divorced while 50% married in 1970 divorced. 11% of children saw their parents divorced in 1950 and 50% of children watched their parents divorce in 1970. Demographer, Nicholas Wolfinger found that there is an intergenerational cycle of divorce and children of divorce are 89% more likely to divorce compared to adults who were raised in intact, married families.
6 Vanessa Martins Lamb, The 1950's and the 1960's and the American Woman: the Transition from the Housewife to the Feminist, History. 2011 <dumas-00680821>. See Notes 1,5,18.
7 www.Safehorizon.org, National Domestic Violence Hotline, 1-800-799-SAFE, Violence, Statistics and Facts. "1 in 4 women will experience domestic violence during their lifetime." History of Battered Women's Movement, Table 1. Herstory of Domestic Violence. www.icadvinc.org.
8 See Notes 1,5,18.

www.blackloveandmarriage.com, James Walsh, Live-In Relationships vs Marriage: The Advantages and Disadvantages of Both, "Couples who live together have a divorce rate 50% higher than those who don't." Live-in arrangements are devoid of commitment vs commitment and stability in marriage. " A family void of commitment is not good for children."
www.firstthings.org. What You Should Know About Living Together. "Couples who participate in a premarital program experience a 30% increase in marital success over those who do not."
9 Hubpages.com Paul Swendson, author, The Ultimate Generation Gap of the 1960s
En.wikipedia.org/wiki/Generation_gap "Baby Boomers seemed to go against everything their parents had previously believed in music, values, governmental and political views."
10 See Notes 1,5,18.
11 See Notes 1,5,18. Discusses how no-fault divorce and the emphasis on the "self-oriented ethic of romance, intimacy, and fulfillment" of the 1960s and 70s changed the landscape of our family relationships from "the prisms of duty" where "intimacy was important, but also child rearing, shared religious faith, mutual spousal aid, a decent job, and a well-maintained home."
12 www.uky.edu Brief History of the Gay and Lesbian Rights Movement in the U.S. – 1969 Stonewall Riot in New York City. sixties-social movements @.wikispaces.com/Gay Liberation, "In the 1960's homosexuality was against the law.
13 En.wikipedia.org/wiki/Lavender marriage. Mixed orientation marriage where one or both partners were homosexual or bisexual. In 1920's in Hollywood there were marriages of convenience known as a Lavender marriage.
 See Note 12.
14 See Note 12.
15 www.yogainternational.com/article/view/tantra-and-the-teachings-of-Abhinavagupta,
16 www.menshealth.com/mhlists/top-sex-secrets/pmtu. php, www.bustle.com/articles/34770-how-long-should-it-take-a-woman-to-come-how-to-stop-worrying-and-start-orgasming, by Vanessa Marin, friendsandlovers.com/for-women-only-htm
17 Hendrix, Harville. Ph.D. *Getting the Love You Want.* New York, NY: Henry Holt Company LLC. 1988
18 www.divorcesource.com/ds/man/u-s-divorce-rates-and-statistics-1037.shtml, www.mckinleyirvin.com/Family-Law-Blog/2012/October/32-Shocking-Divorce-Statistics.aspx, aplus/

com/a/study-marriage-lasts-randy-olson?so=YzuunGbkp6m7zZvK XB2LHL&ref=ns
19   Myss, Caroline, PH.D. *Why People Don't Heal and How They Can*. New York, NY: Three River Press, 1997.
20   The Serenity Prayer written by Reinhold Niebuhr 1892-1971 and adopted by Alcoholics Anonymous and other twelve-step programs. En.wikipedia.org/wiki/Serenity-Prayer
21   Arntz, William; Chasse, Betsy; Vicente, Mark. *What the Bleep Do We Know*. 2007, Used by permission from Health Communications. Inc., Deerfield Beach, Fl.
22   www.staroversky.com/blog/three-minds-consious-subconscious-unconscious, Corsini, R.J. and Wedding, D. Current Psychotherapies (9th ed.). Belmont, Ca: Brooks/Cole, 2011. www.health.harvard.edu/blog/unconscious-or-subconscious
23   www.geniusintelligence.com/nature of the subconsciousmind.htm, www.gurusoftware.com, www.ebtx.com/ntun/ntunsub.htm, www.sacred-texts.com/nth/yfhu/wfhuo6/htm
24   www.johngottman.com and Wikipedia on John Gottman and his Institute. From the 2002 Report. How couples fight and make up.
25   www.robertsrules.com   The Official Robert's Rules of Order Web Site
26   www.firstpeople.us/FP-Html-Legends/TraditionalTalking Stick-Unknown.html
27   Philosophyonthemesa.com/2010/11/01never-apologize-its-a-sign-of-weakness/ by Nina Rosenstand. Quoting an article by Elizabeth Bernstein in the Wall Street Journal about two studies from the University of Waterloo in Ontario, Canada written up in the Journal of Psychological Science.
28   www.quora.com/Why-is-saying-I'm-sorry-a-sign-of-weakness-to-some, www.essense.com/2012/02/28/real-talk-are-apologies-a-sign-of-weakness/,
29   Lyrics by Stephen Stills, www.azlyrics.com/lyricsstephenstills/lovetheoneyourewith.html.
30   Dictionary.reference.com/browse/ego – means self esteem, feelings.
31   Gregg Braden, *The Divine Matrix*. Carlsbad, CA: Hay House, Inc. 2007.
32   Connierae and Tamara Andreas. *Core Transformation*. Moab, Utah: Real People Press, 1994.
33   www.safehorizon.org/page/child-abuse-facts-56.html Child Abuse Facts: 1/3 of those who were abused as children grow up to be abusers of children.

34   Luskin, Dr. Fred, *Forgive for Good, A Proven Prescription for Health and Happiness*. New York, NY: Harper Collins Publishers, Inc., 2002.
Tutu, Desmond. N*o Future Without Forgiveness*. New York, NY: Doubleday Books, 1999.
35   En.wikipedia.org/wiki/Cato-the-Elder/quotes, en.wikipedia.org/wiki/Plutarch, Plutarch was a biographer of Cato the Elder, giving many of his famous quotes. He lived from AD 46-127.
36   www.goodreads.com. Quote by Eleanor Roosevelt. Thedailywayhome.com/achievement-byproduct-happiness-way-around
37   https://www.score.org/
38   Paulo Coelho and Alan R. Clarke. *The Alchemist*. New York, NY: Harper Collins Publishers. 1998.
39   Ncsu.edu/ffci/publications/2008/v14-nl-2008-spring/Washburn-Christensen.php, finance.yahoo.com/news/10-money-mistakes-ruin-marriage-095503587.html Ten Money Mistakes that can Ruin Your Marriage.
40   See Note 37.
41   Orman, Suze. *The Nine Steps to Financial Freedom*. New York, NY: Crown Publishers, 1997
42   www.bloomberg.com/bw/articles/2014-07-17/housings-30-percent-of-income-rule-is-near-useless
43   Compulsive shopping disorder: Jon E. Grant, Christopher B. Donahue, Brian L. Odlaug. *Treating Impulse Control Disorders: A Cognitive-Behavior Therapy Program*. New York, NY: Oxford University Press, 2011. www.healthline.com, www.addictionrecov.org/Addictions/?AID+34, en.wikipedia/wiki/compulsive-buying-disorder, www.indiana.ed/-engs/hints/shop.html, see also Note: 143.
44   En Wikipedia.org/wiki/prenuptual_agreement, www.nolo.com
45   Moneyning.com/housing/the-five-year-rule-for-buying-a-house. Depending on the location of the house matters. Includes not paying closing costs too often. Since you pay interests at first and little towards principal, it comes out about the same as renting until after five years when you'll be paying more on the principal.
46   Orman, Suze. *The Nine Steps to Financial Freedom*. New York, NY: Crown Publishers, 1997
47   Dave Ramsey, www.daveramsey.com, enwikipedia.org/wiki/Dave_Ramsey
48   James Redfield, *The Celestine Prophecy*, New York, NY:

Warner Books, Inc., 1993. Nikki Owen, International Expert in Charisma, https://nikkijowen.com/control-dramas-the-truth-behind-energy-manipulation.

49   Northrup, Christine, M.D. *The Wisdom of Menopause*. New York, NY: Bantam Books, 2001.

50   Chopra, Deepak. *Creating Affluence, The A-to-Z Steps to a Richer Life*. San Rafael, CA: Amber-Allen Publishing, 1998.

51   www.divorcesource.com and Kids Count Data Center. From wwwcensus.gov National Kid Count, American Fact Finder Table C23008. 35% of children under the age of 18 are brought up in single-family homes. From Divorcesource.com and US Divorce Rates and Statistics. There is a high risk for children of divorce and those who live in fatherless homes. 63% of youth suicide, 71% of pregnant teens, 90% of homeless and runaway children, 70% institutionalized, 85% behavioral disorders, 80% rapists, 71% school dropouts, 75% adolescents in chemical abuse centers, 85% youth in prison.

52   See Note 50.

53   Isolina Ricci, Ph.D. *The Co-Parenting Tool Kit: The Essential Supplement for Mom's House*, San Ramon, CA: Custody and Co-Parenting Solutions, 2012. *Dad's House. Mom's House, Dad's House*. New York, NY: Fireside, Simon and Schuster, 1997. *Mom's House, Dad's House for Kids*. New York, NY: Fireside, Simon and Schuster, 2006.

54   Gary Chapman and Ross Campbell. *The Five Love Languages of Children*. Chicago, IL: Norfield Publishing.

55   Connierae and Tamara Andreas. *Core Transformation*. Moab, Utah: Real People Press, 1994.

56   https://www.crystalclarity.com/yogananda/chaper-44/ www.yogamag.net/archives/1983/isep83/gany1.shtml

57   www.goodreaads.com/quote/tag/gandhi, www.patheos.com/blogs/hindu/2015/03/mahatma-gandhi-quotes-inspire/, www.brainyquotes.com/quotes/authors/m/mahatma_gandhi.htmlwww.mindbodygreen.com/0-7059/20-inspiring-quotes-from-mahatma-gandhi.html.

58   Ina May Gaskin, *Spiritual Midwifery*. Summertown, TN: The Book Publishing Co., 1975, and Ina May Gaskin, *Ina May's Guide to Childbirth*, New York, NY: Bantam Dell, 2002.

59   Birth Story: Ina May Gaskin and The Farm Midwives. 2012, birthstorymovie/trailer/

60   The Business of Being Born by Ricki Lake 2008. www.thebusinessofbeingborn.com, www.yidio.com/the-business-of-being-born.com/movies

61   La Leche League started in 1956 is found around the world at www.llli.org and in the US at www.lllusa.org.
62   Ina May Gaskin. *Ina May's Guide to Breastfeeding.* New York, NY: Bantam Books, 2009.
63   Smith, Lendon, Dr., *Feed Your Kids Right*, 1979, *The Encyclopedia of Baby and Child Care*, 1981, *Doctor Mom's Quick Reference Guide to Natural Health Care*, 2000, co-written by Kathy Duerr, All books at Amazon. Com. en.wikipedia.org/wiki/Lendon_Smith
64   Taro Gomi. *Everyone Poops*, Turtleback School and Library Binding edition. Caroline Jayne Church. *Potty Time!* Board Book, 2012, Potty Time Book for Girls, Potty Time Book for Boys, by DK Publishing, 2010. For 14 favorite books on potty training go to www.parents.com/fun/entertainment/books/potty-training-books/#page13.
65   Faber and Mazlish's, *How to Talk to Kids So Kids Will Listen and Listen So Kids Will Talk*, New York, NY: Avon Books, Inc., 1980, Revised 1999
66   Gary Chapman and Ross Campbell. *The Five Love Languages of Children.* Chicago, IL: Norfield Publishing.
67   Description of a Garmin InReach Explorer – www.cabelas.com/Garmin-GPS-Sale
68   www.mayoclinic.org/healthy-lifestyle/children's-health/in-depth, www.psychologytoday.com/screen-time-damages-in-the-brain-screen-time,www.fit.webmd.com/teen/recharge/articles/teens-screen-time, See book: Reset Your Child's Brain by Victoria L. Dunckey, M.D.
69   ldaamerica.org/support/new-to-ld,
70   Statistics from the National Center for Educational Statistics, (2.4 million ld students in the U.S. and 41% of these children receive specialized services,) The National Adult Literacy and Learning Disability Center (60% of adults with severe literacy problems have undetected or untreated ld.) and the National Institute of Health. (75% -80% have trouble with language and reading.) Other resources include: www.pbs.org/parents/readinglanguate/articles/learndis_marco/main.html, www.ldonline.org/article/12836/, - *Life Success For Student with LD: A Parent's Guide.* By Marshall H. Raskind and Roberta J. Goldberg.
71   Ldpride.net/emotions.htm, 33% of children with learning disability are gifted. (buam,1985,brody & mills, 1997, jones, 1986.)
72   Seuss, Dr. *Green Eggs and Ham.* Beginners Book, 1960. Amazon.com
73   yeesata.com, www.facebook.com/yeeatabba, Yee's ATA

Black Belt Academy, Karate for Kids, Modesto, Ca.95355
74   www.newportacademy.com/teenage-hormones-and-sexuality Gonadotropin (GnRH) -releasing hormone triggers pituitary gland to secrete follicle-stimulating hormone (FSH) and luteinizing hormone (LH) in both girls and boys. In girls FSH instructs the ovaries to begin producing estrogen, one of the primary female sex hormones and eggs. En.wikipedia.org/wiki/Comparison-of-birth-control-methods and www.plannedparenthood.org/learn/birth-control/withdrawal-pull-out-method charts to show statistical probability of getting pregnant with all types of birth control or withdrawal method.
75   www.clemson.edu/fyd/Asssets/Adobe_Acrobat_files/tcct-resolving-family-conflict.pdf, www.helpguide.org/article/relationships/conflict-resolution-skills.htm.
76   Conversation with Geary Ritchie, Baja Sur, Ca. 2013.
77   en.m.wikipedia-AFS-Intercultural-Programs.org. en.m.wikipedia.org
78   Barry Spector. *Madness at the Gates of the City: The Myth of American Innocence*. Berkeley, CA: Regent Press, 2010, Angus Ramsey. *Sally's Gift*. Create Space, 2014.
79   Schooloflostborders.org/content/modern-day-rites-of-passage-boysmen-ultimate-form-preventative-medicine, Dr. Ame Rubenstein. Modern Day Rites of Passage for Boys/Men, the Ultimate Form of Preventative Medicine. 04/20/07, en.wikipedia.org/wiki/Rite-of-Passage, www.a partofmanliness.com/2008/11/09/coming-of-age-the-importance-of-male-rites-of-passage.
80   Attwood, Janet and Chris. *The Passion Test, The Effortless Path to Discovering Your Life Purpose*. New York, NY: Penguin Group, 2006.
81   Gleser, Virginia. *Harmony on the High Seas, When Your Mate Become Your Matey*, Modesto, CA: Harmony Publishing, 2011.
82   Connierae and Tamara Andreas. *Core Transformation*. Moab, Utah: Real People Press, 1994.
83   Myss, Caroline, PH.D. *Why People Don't Heal and How They Can*. New York, NY: Three River Press, 1997.
84   Kabat-Zinn, Jon. Wherever You Go, There You Are: Mindfulness Meditation for Everyday Life. New York, NY: Hyperion Books, 1994.
85   Arntz, William; Chasse, Betsy; Vicente, Mark. *What the Bleep Do We Know*. 2007, Used by permission from Health Communications. Inc., Deerfield Beach, Fl.
86   Katie, Byron, *Loving What Is: Four Questions that Can*

Change Your Life. New York, NY: Three Rivers Press, 2002.
Katie, Byron, with Michael Katz. *I Need Your Love – Is That True?* NewYork, NY: Three Rivers Press, 2005
87   www.thepassiontest.com, by Chris and Janet Attwood. *The Passion Test, The Effortless Path to Discovering Your Life Purpose.* New York, NY: The Penguin Group. 2006
88   Rhonda Byrne. *The Secret,* New York: Simon & Schuster, Inc., 2006, and *The Power* (The Secret) 2010.
89   Gregg Braden. *The Divine Matrix.* Carlsbad, CA.: Hay House, Inc. 2007.
90   Chopra, Deepak. *Creating Affluence, The A-to-Z Steps to a Richer Life.* San Rafael, CA: Amber-Allen Publishing, 1998. Dyer, Wayne W. *There's a Spiritual Solution to Every Problem.* New York, Harper Collins Publishers, 2001
Tolle, Eckhart. *A New Earth, Awakening to Your Life's Purpose.* London, England: Penguin Group, 2005.
Tolle, Eckhart. *The Power of Now, A Guide to Spiritual Enlightenment.* Vancouver B. C., Canada: Namaste Publishing, Inc., 1999.
91   www.hayhouse.com, Louise Hay. T*he Power is Within You.* Carlsbad, CA.: Hay House, Inc. 1991. Louise Hay. *You Can Heal Your Life, The Movie*
92   Franquemont, Sharon. Y*ou Already Know What To Do*, New York, NY: Penguin Putnam, Inc., 1999.
93   Real, Terrence. *I Don't Want to Talk About It.* New York, NY: Fireside, 1997
94   Epstein, Lew, Epstein, Francine, Kirkilis, Rebby Epstien. *Trusting You Are Loved.* The Partnership Foundation, 1998, 2014.
95   Hendrix, Harville. Ph.D. *Getting the Love You Want.* New York, NY: Henry Holt Company LLC,1988. Hendrix, Harville. Ph.D. *Keeping the Love You Find.* New York, NY: Atria Books, 1992.
96   Katie, Byron, *Loving What Is: Four Questions that Can Change Your Life.* New York, NY: Three Rivers Press, 2002.
Katie, Byron, with Michael Katz. *I Need Your Love – Is That True?* NewYork, NY: Three Rivers Press, 2005
97   *"Not 'Just Friends': "Rebuilding Trust and Recovering Your Sanity After Infidelity,"* by Shirley P. Glass with Jean Coppock Staehili (2004, Atria Books.)
98   John Money. *Gay, Straight, and In-Between: The Sexology of Sexual Orientation.* New York, NY: Oxford University Press, 1988, Simon LeVay. *The Sexual Brain.* Cambridge, MA: MIT Press, 1993.
99   Joel Crohn, Ph.D. *Mixed Match, How to Create Successful Interracial, Interethnic and Interfaith Relationships.* New York, NY:

Ballantine Books, 1995.
100   Northrup, Christine, M.D. T*he Wisdom of Menopause.* New York, NY: Bantam Books, 2001
Northrup, Christine, M.D. *Women's Bodies, Women's Wisdom.* New York, NY: Bantam Books, 1994
101   Jed Diamond, T*he Irritable Male Syndrome: Managing the Four Key Causes of Depression and Aggression.* Rodale Inc., Roadale Wellness.com. 2005
102   Barbach, Lonnie and Levine, Linda. *Shared Intimacies, Women's Sexual Experiences.* New York, NY: Bantam Books, 1989.
103   National HIV & STD Testing at https://gettested.cdc.gov, and Anonymous testing at www.planned parenthood.org/learn/stds/std-testing-hiv-safer-sex/hiv-aids/hiv-testing and free STD testing at www.freestdcheck.org.
104   Lerner, Harriet Goldhor. Ph.D. *The Dance of Anger.* New York, NY: Harper and Row Publishers, 1985
105   Gary Chapman and Ross Campbell. *The Five Love Languages of Children.* Chicago, IL: Norfield Publishing. 2012 Gary Chapman. *The Other Side of Love.* Chicago IL: Moody Press. 1999.
106   Hendrix, Harville. Ph.D. *Getting the Love You Want.* New York, NY: Henry Holt Company LLC., 1988.
107   Faber and Mazlish's, *How to Talk to Kids So Kids Will Listen and Listen So Kids Will Talk*, New York, NY: Avon Books, Inc., 1980, Revised 1999
108   Leman, Dr. Kevin. K*eeping Your Family Together When the World is Falling Apart.* New York, NY: Delacorte Press, 1992
Leman, Dr. Kevin. *The Birth Order Book, Why You Are the Way You Are.* Grand Rapids, MI: Revell Publishing, 2009
109   Coleman, Joshua, Ph.D. *When Parents Hurt, Compassionate Strategies When You and Your Grown Child Don't Get Along.* New York, NY: Harper Collins Publishers, Inc., 2008.
110   Luskin, Dr. Fred, *Forgive for Good, A Proven Prescription for Health and Happiness.* New York, NY: Harper Collins Publishers, Inc., 2002.
111   Orman, Suze. T*he Nine Steps to Financial Freedom.* New York, NY: Crown Publishers, 1997
112   Dave Ramsey, www.daveramsey.com, enwikipedia.org/wiki/Dave_Ramsey
113   Adult Survivors of Child Abuse at www.naasca.org/010111-Recovery.htm, www.psychecentral.com, www.Isurvive.org, www.adultchildren.org, Rape, Abuse and Incest national Network at http:/www/rainn.org/adult-survivors-of-childhood-sexual-abuse. http://mainweb-v-musc.edu/

vawprevention/general/saunders.pdf, www.health right360.org/ what-we-do-summery-of-programs, fsa-cc.org/survivors-healing-center/, naasca.org/Groups-Services, www.pandy's.org/articles/innerchild.html/ by Melinda, Healing Your Inner Child after Sexual Abuse, wwwlucidpages.com/healing.html. - Healing from Childhood Sexual Abuse. Ellen Bass and Laura Davis. *The Courage to Heal: A Guide for Women Survivors of Child Sexual Abuse.* New York, NY: Harper Collins Publishers, Inc., 1994. Wendy Meltz. *The Sexual Healing Journey.* New York, NY: Harper Collins, 1991. Robin D. Stone. *No Secrets, No Lies: How Black Families Can Heal from Sexual Abuse.* Harmony Publisher. 2007. Support services: www.aftersilence.org, www.ascasupport.org, www.psychecentral.com, www.havoca.org.

114   Katie, Byron and Mitchell, Stephen. *Loving What Is: Four Questions That Can Change Your Life.* New York, NY: Three Rivers Press, 2002.

Katie, Byron, with Michael Katz. *I Need Your Love – Is That True?* New York, NY: Three Rivers Press, 2005.

115   Coleman, Joshua, Ph.D. *When Parents Hurt, Compassionate Strategies When You and Your Grown Child Don't Get Along.* New York, NY: Harper Collins Publishers, Inc., 2008.

116   Luskin, Dr. Fred, *Forgive for Good, A Proven Prescription for Health and Happiness.* New York, NY: Harper Collins Publishers, Inc., 2002.

More Books By Virginia Gleser

Tie-Dye! The How-To Book
User-friendly instructions to create unique and beautiful tie-dye designs.
Over 20,000 copies in print.

Harmony on the High Seas, When Your Mate Becomes Your Matey
Virginia's guide to successful cruising.
Sailing becomes a metaphor for life.

How to Find Love and Make It Last, A Practical Guide to Relationships,
Includes the 101 Question Compatibility Test
Book 1

Chances for a successful relationship improves when you do the work that makes you into a dynamic and compatible partner.

Collaborative Works by Virginia Gleser

Voices of the Farm
Adventures in Community Living

Chapter, The Yellow Canary

Tales from members of The Farm, An Intentional Spiritual Community, Summertown, TN, describing the 12 year, collective experience of the largest commune in the United States.
1970-1983

The Roots of Plenty
Tales from the "hippie peace corps"

Chapter, Plenty Age and Youth Center, Miami, Florida

Stories about the early years of The Farm's non-profit organization, Plenty, International. From the highlands of Guatemala to the South Bronx, inner-city Miami, Haiti, and the Pine Ridge Reservation, etc., Plenty dealt with ambulance services, nutrition, gardening, earthquake reconstruction, etc. Plenty continues its work today.

215

www.ingramcontent.com/pod-product-compliance
Lightning Source LLC
Chambersburg PA
CBHW070657100426
42735CB00039B/2173